When Love Calls You Home

When Love Calls You Home

A Journey to Healing and Restoration

ANNE-MARIE L. JAMES-HENRY

Xulon Press

Xulon Press
2301 Lucien Way #415
Maitland, FL 32751
407.339.4217
www.xulonpress.com

1st Edition: 2022
Send Enquiries to Anne-Marie L. James-Henry
Phone: 1 (240) 374-6884
e-mail: annielhenry@gmail.com

Paperback ISBN-13: 978-1-66285-798-0
Ebook ISBN-13: 978-1-66285-799-7

Dedication

To my husband Marlon whose love called me home from across the oceans to his heart and our home.

Thank you for your love which healed and restored me bringing me into a place of peace and renewed purpose.

I love you so much.

In Memory of

My brothers with a heart of worship: called home to glory.
Barry James whose promotion to glory was one of the catalysts of
my journey.

February 19, 2012

Rev. Berth James whose promotion to glory came at the
culmination of the seventh year of my journey while editing
this book.

January 17, 2021

Rest safely in the arms of the Saviour my brothers and see you
at the heavenly celebration of the saints.

Acknowledgment

I am thankful to Almighty God, Jesus Christ, and Holy Spirit, who is my salvation, rock, and helper. The one who restored my soul, healed my body, sustains me and provided the spiritual insight and grace to complete a second book.

To my, God-sent husband for your love, confidence, support, and encouragement to complete this writing.

Thank you, Apostle Emanuel Vivian Duncan for writing the foreword and pointing me toward a divine pathway in my time of crisis.

Thank you, Arlene Clarke, for assisting with the initial editing and using your keen insight to fine-tune the layout and design.

Thank you, Shakir James (SJ Prolific) my dear nephew for the inspiration for designing the book cover and for doing an exceptional job. You are undoubtedly gifted. To my niece Shanae for your love, encouragement, and support.

To Prophet Joel and Minister Amryl Reuben (Speak Life International) whose prophetic insight became a catalyst for a finisher's anointing and the grace to complete this book.

Thanks to family, friends, and colleagues who encouraged and supported me to complete this second book and tell my story of God's healing and restoration. You gave me hope and held up my hands. I tell my story to you also.

Foreword

I am quite sure at some time or the other that you have heard and even proclaimed the statement, "**Home is Where the Heart Is**". However, have you ever taken the time to truly explore and grasp the dimensions of its meaning? Well, the quest to do so was the first thing that began to resonate in my spirit, when I took on the challenge to prepare the foreword for this book: *When Love Calls You Home – A Journey to Healing and Restoration.*

The parable of **The Prodigal Son** is the story of the young man who left his home which we can call the Heart Of My Existence loaded with that to which he was entitled, but clueless as to who he was. When one leaves home in that manner the journey will more than likely lead you all the way back home.

In Luke 15:11-27, Jesus tells the parable of a father and his two sons, the younger of whom discovers and claims his inheritance from his father. Soon afterward, he left his home: the Heart Of My Existence, taking his inheritance with him, seeking a new and better life in a far country. Sadly, though, because of living a sheltered life, under the roof of his father, he was not street smart. So, having arrived in that far place, Luke describes the young man as having "wasted his substance with riotous living" (Luke 15:13).

To compound the issue, his self-induced financial and social famine soon collided with one induced by nature itself. Consequently, he soon *"began to be in want"* (Luke 15:14). This unfortunate turn of events drove this well-cultured, Jewish young man to do the unthinkable. According to Luke:

> *And he went and joined himself to a citizen of that country, and he sent him into his fields to feed swine. And he would fain have filled his belly with the husks that the swine did eat: and no man gave unto him (Luke 15:15-16).*

According to Luke 15:17, the impact of this experience was that he had a moment of epiphany, and *'he came to himself.'* The impact of this was the peeling off the false personas with which he had clad himself, since the day he had discovered that to which he was entitled and, subsequently, left the **Heart Of My Existence** (home). In that pivotal moment, he also got a vision of, a passion for, and made a resolve to return to the **Hub Of My Energy** (home). There he could see, in his mind's eye, ... *many hired servants of my father's have bread enough and to spare, and I perish with hunger! I will arise and go to my father* (Luke 15:18).

The inflated ego with which this young man had left home, had so many holes punched into it, that by this time, the loud, painful thud with which his head had hit the proverbial rock bottom, now, rendered him bereft of any pretense. He simply knew that his **Here Every Action Reinforces Togetherness** (heart) was pulsating uncontrollably for his **Hub Of My Energy** (home) and would not mind starting from the bottom rung of the ladder, just as long as his father would show him some measure of acceptance and give him access to his **Heart Of My Existence**. His resolve was indelibly etched in his mind thus:

> *and will say unto him, Father, I have sinned against heaven, and before thee, And am no more worthy to be*

called thy son: make me as one of thy hired servants(Luke 15:18-19).

What will stand eternally in this young man's favour is the fact that, in Luke 15:20, Jesus describes him thus, "*And he arose, and came to his father.*" In so doing, Jesus installs him as the undisputed champion of all returnees. You see, in arising, embarking on, and completing the long journey back to his father, the young man, not only challenged, but also, took on and defeated the entire gang of thieves that rob a great percentage of many well-meaning, penitent souls either freeze at the starting line; collapse along the way or, even more regrettably, make an about-turn to the safety of the very pigpen in which both the stench and inhabitants nauseated the daylights out of them, just the night before. A very abridged list of the members of this gang must include some of the most menacing of them: fear, shame, pride, self-flagellation, and hostile public opinion.

Have you decided to go back home to the **Heart Of My Existence?** Have you started the journey? How far along the way are you? What is your orientation at this moment?

- **Making slow but steady steps towards your goal?** Keep on walking!
- **Attempting to go forward, but looking back?** Consider the pigpen and all its offerings to be under attack by fire and brimstone. Remember Lot's wife!
- **Frozen at the side of the road?** Ramp up the fiery passion to get there and thaw out of that deep freeze, induced by the blast of arctic air, coming from the spirit of fear! (Read 2 Tim.1-7)
- **Just about to re-enter the pigpen?** Turn around now! You have lost the taste for what it offers, and you may not make it out alive, the next time around. (Read Luke 9:62).

- **Have been travelling for a long time but cannot seem to reach the finish line? Be encouraged:** That bend in the road is not the end of the road unless you fail to make the turn. (Read Phil.1-6).

Jesus, being the master storyteller that he is, brings the drama of the young man who answers the call of his **Here Every Action Reinforces Togetherness** (heart) back to his **Heart Of My Existence** (home) with the loud sound of an explosive display of restoration, which should make anyone serious about completing the journey as a returnee, shake off the shackles and make the final leg to his or her **Hub Of My Energy** with a cantor, just as the champion does at the end of a gruelling marathon race.

- **You are expected home.** *But when he was yet a great way off, his father saw him, and had compassion, and ran, and fell on his neck, and kissed him (Luke 15:20).*
- **Confession and self-condemnation are voluntary but not mandatory:** *And the son said unto him, Father, I have sinned against heaven, and in thy sight, and am no more worthy to be called thy son (Luke 15:21).*
- **It's a celebration, restoration, and reinstatement time:** Luke proclaims emphatically: *But the father said to his servants, Bring forth the best robe, and put it on him; and put a ring on his hand, and shoes on his feet: And bring hither the fatted calf, and kill it, and let us eat, and be merry: For this, my son was dead, and is alive again; he was lost and is found. And they began to be merry (Luke 15:22-24).*

As we come to the end of this foreword, I am confident that as the reader your appetite is whet, to delve straight into the main course:

When Love Calls You Home - A Journey to Healing and Restoration prepared for you by author: Rev Anne-Marie L. James-Henry. Be sure to consume it all and may your relationships receive an upshot of vitality that cannot be reversed.

FOREWORD PREPARED BY & DULY PERMITTED
FOR USE BY
APOSTLE EMANUEL VIVIAN DUNCAN
DIVINE DESTINY WORSHIP CENTRE
DIEGO MARTIN
Trinidad, Trinidad and Tobago W. I.
evduncan@yahoo.com
1 868 681 2707

Preface

W hen *Love Calls You Home - A Journey to Healing and Restoration* delves into the heart of my experience from the inception of a medical diagnosis to the culmination of the decision to live life fully - being present at the moment. That period spanned approximately seven years. The seventh year of any dispensation, event, or journey is generally recognized as the period of completion, and the eighth year symbolizes new beginnings. My journey started in October of the first year (2013). I completed writing this book in December 2020, the seventh year. The final draft and initial editing occurred in the eighth year, before publishing in 2022.

You will observe that the ten chapters cover different themes (in chronological order) which discuss experiences associated with those topics. I endeavoured to adequately cover the impact of those experiences, emotionally, spiritually, mentally, socially, and physically. From them, you can glean the lessons learned and how they characterized my discovery of God's unfailing love for me. Each chapter identifies biblical passages, which will help to guide you through the internalizing of those truths and how they relate to your current circumstances.

As you read each chapter, I encourage you to do it with an open mind and spirit. I am not saying that my experience will be yours, and it will never be, but you must understand what God wants you to learn during your journey. A major aspect of what you are experiencing is linked to God's divine purpose for your life. Anyone who knows me knows that I am very passionate about living life purposefully. We must always consult with our designer about our purpose and the lessons gleaned from everything we go through. Even if He does not reveal it, we can trust that as our creator, He knows what is best for us. If you have a challenge identifying what that looks like you can refer to my first book *The Seasons of Your Life*.

When Love Calls You Home - A Journey to Healing and Restoration was written for those who are on a journey of restoration and healing. It encompasses those who struggle to find meaning in their lives and surmount the challenges of daily living, which weigh them down beneath the noises of the masses to conform to the status quo. I also write to all my sisters searching for love who doubt the possibility of it happening because of injured mindsets, personal limitations, cultural beliefs, and unhealthy spiritual bondage. Know that with God all things are possible if you can only believe and trust His heart and love for you.

My prayer is that as you read this authentic expression of my heart and experiences, written from a place of vulnerability and transparency, you can find hope that God sees you, understands you, and change is possible.

Rev Anne-Marie L. James Henry, BTH, MCC, MMFT

Author

Minister, Marriage and Family Therapist, Life Coach,

Military Spouse

Table of Contents

Introduction

The Lord has appeared of old to me, saying: "Yes, I
have loved you with an everlasting love; Therefore with
lovingkindness, I have drawn you."

(Jer. 31:3)

When you encounter true love, it draws you into its circle.
Though it may be difficult to define that experience we know
it is best when embraced and genuinely expressed by the giver. I always
say, true love always seeks the highest good of the other person and
expects nothing in return. I experienced the unfailing and unending
love of God in the middle of a difficult period of my life. Yes, the
experiences which precipitated the transitions were challenging but
they revealed God and the nature of my relationship with Him that
will be unforgettable.

Our Heavenly Father's love has the nature of sacrifice and He
asked us to pattern His love in our relationships. From the time man
sinned God's redemptive plan for mankind was activated (Gen. 3:1-
24). Since then, reconciliation of man into the right relationship with
Him was on God's mind and Jesus Christ became the visible manifestation of that divine plan and love.

The name of this book *When Love Calls You Home - A Journey
to Healing and Restoration* was given to me by God before I had my

crisis experience. At the time I did not know that I would go through that challenging season, which would define God's love for me and my love for others. This experience eventually introduced me to my husband in an unconventional and out-of-character manner, and only after that time, I was able to start writing. ***When love Calls You Home - A Journey to Healing and Restoration*** depicts the relationship God wants to have with us generally, but primarily in the difficult moments or seasons of our lives, when we feel like God is not there and no one cares. It highlights His loving intent to bring us into true intimacy with Him, through the insurmountable and negative circumstances of our lives. It is an inspirational discourse about restoration and finding purpose through life's difficulties.

The first vision and prodding I received for the book was a reflection on the parable of the Prodigal Son's experience taught by Jesus Christ in the Gospel of Luke found in the New Testament (Luke 15:11-32). The Father's love can transcend any situation or geographical boundary and transport us to the place of God's ultimate destiny and desire for us. There are no limitations to that love. I learned that for some of us, we will go through that rocky road and those turbulent waters before we get to that place of divine understanding, access, and embracing of His love. Eventually, we will obtain victory and rest, in Christ, because we chose to subsume that love. In that place, the love of God enfolds us like a cloak that protects us from the latent effects of the journey and pulls us into the comfort of His grace and calling on our lives.

A process is never a pretty picture. Imagine a house under reconstruction or someone who was scarred from a fire or car wreck and must undergo plastic surgery. Hopelessness turns to celebration when they see the final product. Well, it is the same for lives under reconstruction. It is a journey, and the final product will always surprise you.

A journey is a process that involves moving towards the intended destination. Though there may be times of uncertainty that can give way to immobility, there may be other actions occurring simultaneously like mental activity. The word journey reflects traveling from one place to another.[1] A journey may or may not have a stipulated culminating time, but the important objective is to reach the destination. I am yet to see a journey that goes in a straight line. A journey always holds the possibility of dangerous experiences where there are twists, turns, bumps, bridges, detours, stops, slows, slips, and accidents. Life is a journey, and you can find all those descriptions of a journey in your life. We cannot be delusional about the possibility of the outcome if the traveller does not have an intentional plan. Some people survive, some die along the way, some end the expedition prematurely with scars, bruises, and bumps, while others arrive successfully with the scars to celebrate the victory.

Healing is a process that may be painful sometimes. You cannot rush it, especially emotional brokenness, trauma, and grief. Healing as a process involves making or becoming sound again.[2] One of God's desires for His children is healing (3 John 1:2). The Bible is replete with instances of healing from the Old Testament to the New Testament (Genesis 20:17; 2 Kings 5:1-19; 2 Chronicles 30:20; Psalm 103:2-5; Proverbs 3:7-8; Jeremiah 30:17; 1 Peter 4:10). The gift of healing is one of the spiritual gifts manifested in the New Testament Church and should be operational among believers today (Luke 9:1; 1 Corinthians 12:30; 14:1-40). In the Old Testament, healing occurred solely as an act of God as He gave the directive to His prophets and servants. In the New Testament, healing operates through the ministerial offices given to the Church as a gift of the Holy Spirit and can manifest through any believer, who possesses the gift of healing.

The references to healing in Scripture are not only a physical phenomenon but also imply emotional healing. God promised to heal the broken-hearted person.

He heals the brokenhearted and binds up their wounds (Ps. 147:3).

Healing can be both instantaneous and gradual. There are times when healing happens as a supernatural act of God and the person receives a miracle. Some people receive healing through a medical procedure or physical and mental health therapy. However, we must be careful to distinguish between the supernatural, miraculous acts of God and the therapeutic methods through which one can receive catharsis when illnesses and diseases are ameliorated by human intervention.

Restoration happens with an earnest desire for change from a negative circumstance to a former position of wholeness. Restoration implies the reinstatement of a former place, position, quality, condition, or state.[3] The word **restoration** is a combination of the prefix **re** and the transitive verb **store.** The prefix **re -** means **again, anew,** or **back,** depending on the context in which it is used.[4] To store is to layaway, furnish, supply, or source.[5] The definition implies that we are inherently storehouses of both positivity and negativity. For the believer, we are spiritual storehouses of God's power and presence because we are the temple of the Holy Ghost. Sometimes the storehouse can become depleted, but we must recognize when we need to restock. God comes to us (or as we go to Him) and restores our storehouses to the original position so that we would return to our former position of fullness and wholeness. The Psalmist David highlights the role of God in restoring our souls:

He restores my soul; He leads me in the paths of righteousness for His name's sake (Ps. 23:3).

I already implied that restoration of a building is always more difficult than erecting a new one. Restoration says there is value in the previous design, but the modifications would create a new masterpiece and the refurbishment would reinstate hope and purpose. God wants to restore hope and purpose in your life, just as He did for me.

In this book, I used my experiences to share how God used a crisis to reposition me for my next season. A season in which I now walk. A season of healing and restoration. He shifted me from one global location to another and changed my identity and vocation. He placed a strong man in my life who provided and helped me through this transition. God redirected my life and used me like Joseph to pave the way for others in my family. What the enemy meant for evil God turned it around for His good, and I am continuing in my journey of healing and restoration.

As I am writing and completing this book in the anniversary month and the seventh year after this experience, I am grateful and overcome with wonder. How fitting because seven is the number of completion and I never thought I would live beyond the immediacy of the experience. My transition demonstrates the awesome power of God to determine the outcome of every experience in our lives when we walk in obedience and allow Him to direct our steps.

It is my prayer that as you read, your life would be renewed, refreshed, and revived. I desire that you would appreciate God's work in your life as He shifts and changes the courses and seasons that surround you. That you will experience the grace and love of God to usher you supernaturally from the crisis to your destiny. To walk into a boundless love, which you will discover as you read the pages of, **When Love Calls You Home - A Journey to Healing and Restoration.**

> *"Remember, there are no real failures in life, only results. There are no true tragedies, only lessons. And there really are no problems, only opportunities waiting to be recognized as solutions by the person of wisdom."*

> -Robin Sharma

CHAPTER 1

Crisis for a Conviction

But may the God of all grace, who called us to His eternal glory by Christ Jesus, after you have suffered a while, perfect, establish, strengthen, and settle you.

(1 Pet. 5:10)

Seasonal crises are normal in life whether it is personal, family, church, and career. I also faced those crisis experiences but this one "rocked my world," so to speak. And given my state of mind, I had to make a fundamental decision about my faith in the Lord Jesus Christ. On this journey, I heard God distinctly ask me, **"Will you trust me in this?"**

A crisis can define your conviction about self, others, beliefs, and values. It creates an atmosphere where you can inevitably make a critical decision to continue your existence. Not merely as a human being but as a person created by God with a pre-ordained destiny. That was my position in October of 2013. A crisis that started after the diagnosis continued for two years. Eventually, I continued to walk in faith and acceptance of the Father's will after eight years. This experience changed the course of my destiny beyond my most sane beliefs. I reached a crossroads, and it became my turning point.

There are several initial responses that someone can exhibit in a crisis including panic, fear, confusion, guilt, hopelessness, and blame. Each reaction depends on the known or assumed cause of the crisis. My initial reaction was confusion and blame. Confusion because I thought I had the formula for ensuring that I did not get such a bad medical report and there I was, and this happened to me. "But I did everything right," I said to myself. "I may not be a saint, but I tried to do right by God." I blamed myself for not observing the signs that I was stressed and burnt out and worked hard but was not smart. I reasoned that I should have taken better care of myself while I was taking care of everyone else. At that time, I was employed full-time as a facilitator of a values education program at secondary school, assistant pastor of a congregation of approximately 100 members, a lecturer at a theological college, a mentor with a national mentorship program, a pastoral and community counsellor, and pursuing a master's degree.

There was a sign that something was happening with my body. I observed the change one day as I made my way to the educational facility for my studies in Trinidad, which was located on a hill. When I attempted to walk up the hill to the building, I could not proceed without stopping periodically, since I was breathless. There were stairs in the building leading to the classrooms, and again I stopped midway while climbing the stairs. I knew something was wrong but felt it was tiredness or I needed to lose some weight.

Sometime after that discovery, I scheduled a routine visit with my primary care physician. I was feeling more tired than usual lately, my feet were swelling, the shortness of breath continued, and I was having some back pain. As I sat in the doctor's office I started crying while relating how I felt. I also told him that my family had four deaths in two years and with the grief and all I was doing maybe my body was tired. He decided to check for any uterine infection, referred me for an ultrasound, both abdominal and pelvic, gave me some medication for the swelling of the feet, and sent me on my way.

I went to my ultrasound appointment the following week and while conducting the ultrasound the radiologist started asking me some questions which I considered to be strange. Do you have high blood pressure? Are you diabetic? Do you have kidney problems? Are you in pain? All my responses were, "No!" Then, I heard her say to her assistant who was busy typing the report, *"right renal artery aneurysm."* I said to myself, "That sounds pretty serious." Then the procedure ended. After returning home from the appointment, I did not go to Google but grabbed the faithful old medical dictionary on the bookshelf, opened the report, and looked for the definition of each word in that report. "Well," I said to myself. "This sounds serious." And it was.

I took the report back to my doctor the following day. He looked at me in disbelief. I asked him, "Where did that come from?" his response was, "Who knows." He further explained that it was difficult to determine the origins if a patient does not have the conditions which will predispose them to that medical condition. Then he said what was more important was that the diagnosis is known early before anything further happened to me. He told me if the aneurysm ruptured, I could get a heart attack, or my body could go into shock. That meant I could bleed to death or damage my kidneys, without immediate medical attention. I was perplexed and started crying. He said I should not worry, and he will give me a referral to see a specialist. I was referred to a nephrologist (kidney specialist) - it was the first time I heard the word. My doctor told me some stories of individuals whose lives were saved in the nick of time while doing routine examinations. He said to me, "You are a lucky woman, and someone is watching over you." He further instructed me to tell my family what was going on so that if anything happened, they would know what to do - which would be to rush me to a hospital immediately. **CRISIS**!

How could I tell my family the news when I lost my youngest brother suddenly to liver cancer at the age of 37 in February of the previous year? My mother was overseas to attend the funerals of her sister and brother-in-law. The family was still grieving so I knew that news of my medical condition would crush them. Death, especially the sudden death of family members can have devastating effects on other family members who attempt to manage the loss. It causes trauma, which if not managed can have severe consequences for family members. I decided to refrain from disclosing the information until I knew what next to do. For three months I said nothing to anyone and did not visit the doctor again until after that time. Why? I needed a word from the Lord, I had to get my spirit settled about what to do, and I was desperate.

I began searching for an explanation for the aneurysm and previously asked the doctor if a fall could contribute to the diagnosis. He responded that there may be a possibility. I spent some time reflecting and researching the possible reasons for my diagnosis. While I researched the medical information, I remembered the instances when I fell, which I thought could have contributed to my physical condition. When I attended theological college, I fell after taking a bath and stepped on a mat when exiting the bathroom. I injured my back and left knee. My right leg went forward while my left knee bent behind my back since I stepped out with the right leg first. The doctors at the medical facility told me the ligaments in my knee were torn. I could not walk without aid for a week and did some therapy on the knee and currently continue to have pains in my knee. The second and third time I fell was on the stairs in my workplace. The first time was not serious but the second time I injured my ankle and hit the right side of my body on the stairs. I could not walk for two days but did not take it seriously.

In January 2014 I decided to see the referred specialist (nephrologist). A day before my appointment with the nephrologist, I spoke to another doctor who is a Christian, and she asked to see me at her office. She said, "Anne-Marie there must be some good to come out of this because this cannot be logically or medically understood or explained, but it is serious." She further said, "It is rare that you will have an aneurysm in the right renal artery." If you are reading this and you still do not understand, imagine three arteries leading to each kidney. The aneurysm was in the arteries leading to the right kidney. It is a swelling, small bulge, or balloon-like object over the arteries.

When I visited the specialist, my blood pressure was higher than normal 165/95. That was new for me since my vitals were always lower than normal and as a person who was considered slightly anemic, that was cause for concern. My blood count was 8, definitely below normal. It was as though my body was doing whatever it wanted to do. The specialist was also baffled about my diagnosis. I enquired if she encountered any patient with that medical condition during her practice. She responded that she knew of only one male patient who decided against surgery, and as far as she knew, he was still alive. I was given referrals to see a vascular surgeon. Then she told me I should not make any hasty decision about having surgery, since my condition was unusual in the medical field.

When I left the doctor's appointment at the hospital in Tobago that day, I felt deflated. I asked myself "What am I going to do?" Then, I heard the voice of God in my spirit man speaking to me, **"Do not let any doctor touch your body for surgery. I will fix you myself."** Huh! That moment was the first time I knew that this was a situation for God. I will talk more about this in the next chapter. However, at that time I had to consciously clarify my Christian beliefs and conviction of who God was and is in my life. I concluded that it was better to obey the voice of God rather than man. I made that decision for several reasons apart from being fearful. The journey was new to me, the doctors did not know what was happening. There was no convincing theory about my medical condition, the situation was volatile and complicated, and I could not place my family in another situation of grief because I made a wrong decision that will cause them to lose me or take care of me for the rest of their lives. The crisis continued.

WHAT IS A CRISIS?

Let me first define a crisis for you. The word crisis means *to decide*. Its root is in both Greek and Latin. From which you derive the following meanings:[6]

- ✦ the turning point for better or worse in an acute disease or fever
- ✦ paroxysmal attack of pain, distress, or disordered function
- ✦ an emotionally significant event or radical change of status in a person's life
- ✦ the decisive moment
- ✦ an unstable or crucial time or situation in which a decisive change is impending, (especially one with the distinct possibility of a highly undesirable outcome)
- ✦ a situation that has reached a critical phase

We can conclude that a crisis is any event or situation which significantly hinders and inhibits normal functioning. It eventually creates distress and averts the desire to achieve one's goals.

DEFINITION OF CONVICTION

I must also define conviction[7] since it is included in the title of this chapter, and I want you to get a clear understanding of the conviction the crisis ignited within me.

A conviction is

+ an act or process of convicting a crime, especially in a court of law.
+ the act of convincing a person of error or of compelling the admission of truth, the state of being convinced of error or compelled to admit the truth.
+ a strong persuasion or belief, the state of being convinced, certainty, or opinion.

CRISIS DECISIONS

In a time of crisis, it is difficult to continue with the status quo or business as usual. It is also important to refrain from making impulsive decisions since what is at stake is not only personal but there is always a collective impact for those associated with the person in crisis. When nations enter a crisis there is always a sound, a call to attention, a battle cry, or mobilization of the troops. I discovered that in any event of a crisis the first strategy is to engage the attention of all personnel directly involved in the crisis. One should also incorporate those who possess the capabilities and credentials or authority to make a decision. Nothing remains the same, and everyone becomes fixated on how to interface, intervene, and deescalate the crisis. When that happens, it requires investigation, planning, strategizing, and careful consideration of the next move. It is never a time to vacillate, but one must be certain about how to get to a better place beyond the current circumstances, to benefit those affected. Educating and normalizing are some of the first intervention tasks in a crisis.[8] My focus? I needed to know the mind of God and what He required of me.

I had to make some decisions and it started with disengaging from all major responsibilities for a season. I will admit that I loved what I was doing, but what I was doing did not love me at the moment. It was taking a toll on me spiritually, mentally, emotionally, psychologically, and manifested physically. Making those difficult decisions measured my allegiance to service or God, pleasing others, or loving myself more. A defining moment of vocation, calling, and purpose. Note here that I started working at age nineteen, entered theological college at age twenty-one, started full-time ministry at age twenty-five, and continued working until that diagnosis. Keep in mind that as a teenager I was involved in Church activities from age fourteen when I was saved and gave it my all because I felt it was normal for a Christian to always occupy one's time in service for God. Holidays and self-care were not a priority. Therefore, even though I took time off throughout the years the holidays were always interspersed with ministerial activities. Those activities included kid's crusades, women's conferences, mission trips, Daily Vacation Bible School (DVBS), training activities, and anything else that added to my service in the kingdom. My involvement in non-profit organizations and self-advancement with academic pursuits always continued because I had a drive and a love for service and people. In retrospect, I feel like I did not pay enough attention to self-care, which I will talk more about later. I realized that I did too much and had to let a lot go when I received the diagnosis of a right renal artery aneurysm.

I released the responsibility as a lecturer at the theological school and took a sabbatical from ministerial activities which limited my responsibilities as an assistant pastor. I also gave up responsibilities as a mentor with the Trinidad and Tobago Ministry of National Security mentoring program and declined counseling appointments. Changes continued by declining every invitation for a ministerial appointment or request for ministry or service. I shelved the pursuit of a master's degree in Family Life Education. The only position I retained was my job, with limited responsibilities working from the office and supervising rather than working directly within a stressful school setting.

The purpose of a crisis is to measure your ability to define the boundaries of your life and relationships. It determines your true personality and how you will manage yourself and your relationship with others when you feel overwhelmed. Will you crumble or stand strong? Which in effect legitimizes your beliefs and the foundations which held you in a sturdy position during the previous years of your life. It is a test of your resilience and rectitude about life, yourself, and others. Whether you want to engage in the process or not, it happens because of the choices you make, and how you prioritize those decisions at that time. There is always difficulty before achievement, but at the crossroads, you must make some critical life-changing decisions. Those decisions reinforce your honesty about what is most important at that time when the crisis occurs. *You are not alone in your crisis!* God is with you and will direct your path so that you can achieve your God-designed purpose. The crisis you are experiencing will not overtake you, you can get through this season, and you will achieve your victory. Do not be anxious or afraid because of a bad report or an unexpected detour in your journey.

CHAPTER 2

Specimen for His Glory

The word which came to Jeremiah from the Lord, saying: "Arise, and go down to the potter's house, and there I will cause you to hear my words." Then I went down to the potter's house, and there he was, making something at the wheel. And the vessel that he made of clay was marred in the hand of the potter; so he made it again into another vessel, as it seemed good to the potter to make. Then the word of the Lord came to me saying: "O house of Israel, can I not do with you as this potter?" says the Lord. "Look, as the clay is in the potter's hand, so are you in My hand, O house of Israel!"

(Jer. 18:1-6)

NO DESPAIR NO GLORY

At the beginning of my journey, while at home in Tobago, one day I was meditating about the doctor's diagnosis and heard these words from the Holy Spirit. "Anne-Marie the purpose of this physical challenge - this sickness, is so that you will be a specimen for my glory." When I heard the words the tears flowed. I felt like I had been through so many difficult situations in life, and I was tired. I felt the weight of the world on my shoulders and I carried more than my human frailty could contain. I questioned, "What did I do wrong? Why should this happen to me?" There was some self-blame. Then I started asking again, "Is it because I walked in disobedience? Is it because I failed God at times?" There was the guilt talking now. Then I started saying, "Lord if you are ready for me, take me home. It is okay, just give me some time to get some things together. I will be ready." There was the self-pity talking. I continued, "How will my family take this? My parents just lost a son, they cannot deal with losing me now. What will they do without me?" That was my innate fear engaged in talking words of doubt. Myriads of emotional responses happened at the same time, and they swallowed me. Without a clear vision of what I needed to do at that moment, I was lost, and the emotions engulfed me.

When I heard the Holy Spirit speaking, it created a moment of realization and placed the emotional turmoil in perspective. I realized I was like clay in the hand of a master craftsman. Like the prophet Jeremiah in the Old Testament (Jer. 18) I was about to experience the absolute power and sovereignty of Almighty God who possessed the ability to carry me through this unknown season.

THE PROCESS

I entered a process of reshaping likened to that of clay in the hands of a potter. Perhaps you may not understand the role of a potter so let me explain. Pottery is one of the oldest and most widespread decorative arts, consisting of objects made of clay and hardened with heat. The objects made are commonly useful ones, such as vessels for holding liquids, or plates and bowls from which one can serve food.[9]

Pottery making is not a universal craft and is rarely found among nomadic tribes since potters must live within reach of their raw materials. Moreover, if there are gourds, skins, and similar natural materials that can be made into vessels without trouble, there is no incentive to make pottery. It was common among the Jews for many of them to be engaged in this skill. At the time of Jeremiah's writing in chapter 18, the Jews were held captive by the Assyrians who were also practitioners of this trade. An allegory was used by God to identify a familiar cultural practice to reveal spiritual truths to Jeremiah. God wanted him to understand what He will do with His people in that season. When God spoke to Jeremiah, the word of the Lord about the fate of Judah in the hands of the Assyrians came to Jeremiah as an object lesson as he obeyed God and visited the potter's house.

> *Then the word of the Lord came to me, saying: "O house of Israel, can I not do with you as this potter?" says the Lord. "Look, as the clay is in the potter's hand, so are you in My hand, O house of Israel!"(Jer. 18:5-6).*

Like the house of Judah and the people of Jerusalem, I was just clay in the hands of God, I was not a finished product. I was not a whole, complete, beautiful specimen to admire and just scoop up to be carried home and placed as an ornament on a shelf. *no!* There was still work to be done and the crisis experience became the catalyst through which God would work to make me ready to receive His unconditional love for my next assignment.

The metaphorical language used about the potter in the Bible usually carried two meanings: judgment on the wicked, or restoration of the righteous. The judgment of God in the potter's house analogy can be found in the Psalms.

You shall break them with a rod of iron; You will dash them to pieces like a potter's vessel (Ps. 2:9).

In Jeremiah Chapter 18 the mission was restorative. The directive was purposeful to bring the children of Israel into their divine inheritance and demonstrate to the other nations that they were a nation called and appointed by God. The distinct picture which the metaphor presents is one that directed Jeremiah to also understand that a potter can determine how to shape and refine the clay to achieve the best product. Similarly, the love of God will not allow us to remain the same, and He always seeks to align us into an image that reflects more of Him daily.

There are some specific elements that a potter usually needs to create a refined product. They are the potter's wheel, water, and fire. The wheel helps to shape the clay into the desired vessel. The water is needed to make the clay malleable and workable so that the vessel is more defined as it begins to take shape. The clay particles cannot become cohesive without water, so the water softens and binds the clay. When the potter finishes the vessel, it was usually baked in a kiln at temperatures as high as 2700 degrees F. This was necessary because it measured the strength of the vessel to resist high temperatures and not crumble with the slightest exposure to heat. Did you know that before forming the vessel, the clay was usually trampled under feet, kneaded, prodded, twisted, and turned in different directions to soften it and create cohesion before the potter *slaps* it on the potter's wheel for shaping? If that does not happen before it is formed, then with the slightest contact with heat it will easily fall apart. Visualize yourself as clay. God is always at work to shape us more like Him and His intention toward us is good. Though the trials and the difficulties you face may be a weight on your life and you feel that you would be consumed by those trials, God is going to do His complete work to bring you into your purpose. I had to envision that my Savior was involved in a process of shaping me through the crisis. He planned to create within me what was needed to bring me into the fulness of His design for my life. If you are currently experiencing a crisis, know that your God - the designer, is at work to create a beautiful masterpiece because you are a *designer's original.*

> *Beloved, do not think it strange concerning the fiery trial which is to try you, as though some strange thing happened to you; but rejoice, to the extent that you partake of Christ's sufferings, that when His glory is revealed, you may also be glad with exceeding joy (1 Pet. 4:12-13).*

THE HOLY SPIRIT AS CLEANSING WATER AND PURIFYING FIRE

The Bible describes the Holy Spirit as water and fire. That speaks to the work that the Holy Spirit does in the life of the believer. Water and fire mirror the purifying and cleansing work of the Holy Spirit that invades our lives to purify and sanctify us as vessels of God. They are the figurative vehicles of the lasting spiritual change that all believers need so they can grow in their spiritual journey and stand strong during trials and tribulations. That does not mean that there is an absence of other spiritual tasks to accomplish in a believer's life. It is one aspect of the spiritual work that Christ performs in their lives through the Holy Spirit.

> *For by one Spirit, we were all baptized into one body-whether Jews or Greeks, whether slaves or free-and have all been made to drink into one Spirit (1 Cor. 12:13).*

CLEANSING WATER

The work of the Holy Spirit begins from the moment a person receives Christ into their life. When they receive him, the Spirit indwells them and begins to perform the transformative work which every believer requires to live a victorious Christian life. There is no distinction or discrimination about who has access to the purifying work of the Holy Spirit. Jesus Christ constantly calls the believer to access this purification which is available to all who believe and will receive it. Though we cannot tell God how to work in us - because He is the potter, we know He already provided His gift of the Holy Spirit, to help us achieve the goal of purification.

> *On the last day, that great day of the feast, Jesus stood and cried out, saying, "If anyone thirsts, let him come to Me and drink. He who believes in Me, as the Scripture has said, out of his heart will flow rivers of living water." But this He spoke concerning the Spirit, whom those who believe in Him would receive; for the Holy Spirit was not yet given because Jesus was not yet glorified (John 7:37-39).*

Jesus clarified the work of the Holy Spirit as a source of strength for every believer who may be spiritually thirsty and in need of sustenance from God. Sometimes the cares, struggles, and challenges of this life leave us weary and tired. We become thirsty and hungry, longing for a place or something that can be an oasis for our body, soul, and spirit.

> *For I will pour water on him who is thirsty, And floods on the dry ground: I will pour My Spirit on your descendants, And My blessing on your offspring (Isa. 44:3).*

The living water of the Holy Spirit fills us with a feeling of peace and assurance to provide the strength to continue our journey of life. The word spoken by Jesus declared that as we drink, we receive renewed strength, energy, and determination. We can continue being who He called us to be and press through the burdens which hold us back from accomplishing His will.

> *…. but whoever drinks of the water that I give him will never thirst. But the water that I shall give him will become in him a fountain of water springing up into everlasting life (John 4:14).*

As Jesus spoke to the woman at the well, she received enlightenment that transformed a seemingly impossible situation from death to life. She received spiritual truths which revolutionized her thinking and transported her toward a place of change. She understood the figurative language of water in her desperation for change. Her image of who she was and what she was designed to do created a consequential decision that she expressed in her words and actions when she left the well. That encounter bore evidence of the limitless cleansing work of the Holy Spirit to step into any situation, when invited, and transform our lives. When we experience that encounter, we are never the same. The cleansing work births within us the divine nature of Christ so that we can represent him fully on the earth. We must know when we are in a position of thirst and need to receive the refreshing, cleansing power of the Holy Spirit. We must be truthful to ourselves and access what is already available for us to be revived and restored.

PURIFYING FIRE

In the Biblical book of Hebrews, the writer described God as a *"consuming fire."* If *"the fire"* is one of the metaphors used to describe God, then it should not be strange that the same is used to describe the Holy Spirit or the work of the Holy Spirit in the believer's life.

For our God is a consuming fire (Heb. 12:29).

When the Bible describes the Holy Spirit as fire it speaks to the ability to introduce the presence, passion, and purity of God in the body of Christ or the lives of believers. In the Old Testament God used a fire over the tabernacle at night as a symbol of His presence among the nation of Israel as they journeyed through the wilderness (Num. 9:14-15). That fire provided light and guidance along their treacherous journey as they faced their enemies. Within the New Testament Scriptures, the Holy Spirit descended after the ascension of Jesus Christ and dwelled within the believers of the early Church as the temples and tabernacles of the living Christ (2 Cor. 5:1; 6:16). The event of Pentecost, as the Holy Spirit came as tongues of fire and sat upon the heads of the believers, points to the manifestation of the Holy Spirit as fire to ignite a passion and boldness for lifelong service to accomplish the will of God.

> *And when they had prayed, the place where they were assembled together was shaken, and they were all filled with the Holy Spirit, and they spoke the word of God with boldness (Acts 4:31).*

The Holy Spirit as an agent of sanctification purifies us by fire by removing all the impediments, dross, and ungodliness so that we as cleansed vessels can stand in truth and declare, "Thus saith the Lord." We do that without hindrances and guilt knowing that what was spoken will happen because of the cleansing, purifying work of the Holy Spirit in our lives.

> *… who gave Himself for us, that He might redeem us from every lawless deed and purify for Himself His own special people, zealous for good works (Titus 2:14).*

TRIED BY FIRE

There is another profession within scripture used figuratively for the purifying work of God in our lives. That profession is a silversmith who works with iron, steel, or metals. My second brother Berth learned the skill of metal fabricating. Berth started working as an apprentice after secondary school with a metal fabricator in our village. He made objects from iron and steel, and I always found the end products fascinating. I remember visiting the fabricator's shop where my brother worked and observed that they would heat the metals and pound it into the desired shape. Since the iron and steel required extensive heat, they wore protective clothing and safety gear such as gloves and goggles. One day my brother came home with his eyes looking red and said it was hurting, the next day he could not go to work, his eyes were swollen, and he had difficulty seeing. He used an eye drop until he was better before returning to work. I learned about *Arc eyes*[10] and the importance of wearing eye protection, by not staring with the naked eye at the sparks and fire from the heating process when welding the metals. The intense heat was necessary for the metals but not conducive to the eyes. God knows that there are some areas of our lives that require the intense heat of the Holy Spirit to produce change and shape our lives into His image. This process begins with spiritual preparation to receive from the Holy Spirit as he pours out his fire on our lives.

God is likened to a silversmith as He works through His Holy Spirit to make us into His image and likeness. He is the potter or the silversmith that works with the vessel and pushes it through the purifying fire of the Holy Ghost to create a perfect vessel that can stand against the test of time and the fiery darts of the enemy and not be afraid.

> *The refining pot is for silver and the furnace for gold, But the Lord tests the hearts (Prov. 17:3).*

From our discourse, one observes God's revelation to Jeremiah was significant. The statement was given to Jeremiah about what he could do to direct the path of Judah and Jerusalem. He expected their response to be one where they stopped and recognize His ability to shift and change the course of their destiny in any direction He desired.

Through my journey to healing and wholeness, I realized that God was skilfully orchestrating a divine event to bring me to a place of fulfilling His purpose. Though the fiery process was difficult to contain it was a necessary part of my journey. This necessary path helped to cleanse, purify, rekindle the godly passion, and reposition me for His will while revealing the glory of God. God used both the good and bad of my experiences for His glory and determined that I will be a vessel for His praise. **HALLELUJAH!**

CHAPTER 3

Resistance or Resolve

Therefore submit to God. Resist the devil and he will flee from you.

(*James 4:7*)

W hen you enter a strange or unknown territory there will be some feeling of trepidation and uncertainty and when you make a decision, that goes against the norms, there will be resistance. After receiving my diagnosis, I was fearful and knew I had to make some decisions that would take me into uncharted territories. Before the health crisis, I had no major health conditions which needed urgent medical attention or hospitalization. Once I had, a slight case of food poisoning, and I received intravenous fluids in the emergency department of the hospital. During my teen years and into early adulthood I also experienced migraine headaches. After crossing age thirty my only health concerns were menstrual cramps and later fibroids which contributed to an anemic condition. Therefore, the reproductive cycle challenges and low blood count were the only medical situations that needed attention. Annual medical visits were limited to my Obstetrician Gynecologists (OBGYN), primary care physician, dentist, and optician to monitor and maintain routine health.

The diagnosis came at a time when I was like an engine operating on overload without oil. I was tired, exhausted, and needed to rest but my love for what I was doing and taking care of family issues was greater than my attention to self-care. I was burnt out and needed to just **STOP**! Then came some opposition. There was intrinsic and extrinsic resistance. As you can already guess, my struggle to change a norm that I was accustomed to for many years was exacting, but my health was at stake. I reasoned within that I was not expendable, and as one of my friends used to say, "Your replacement is already ordered." I told myself, "Anne-Marie, as much as they love you for what you do when you are gone, they will mourn for a while, and then they will replace you." I realized the power was mine to decide the outcome of my health and life.

As a trained and licensed marriage and family therapist, I understand the impact of emotional pain, trauma, and grief on the mind and body. The body records those events and experiences. *The Body Keeps the Score* emphasizes the effect of trauma on the body which results in post-traumatic stress because of numbing to suppress the memory of overwhelming experiences or traumatic events. This changes the biological stress response and can culminate in anxiety, fear, and dissociation. This forces the emotions to remain in a false sense of control which places the body under stress to suppress memories. When there is a stimulus to trigger the suppressed memories, the body goes into shock which can negatively impact the functioning of various bodily systems (Van Der Kolk, 1994).[11] It is very important to seek help for any traumatic experience, grief, or loss of any kind.

Initially, it was difficult to decide to relinquish all the roles and responsibilities I carried. I later realized that it was because I was a "people pleaser." How could I not be? As someone raised in the Christian Church and taught that service is the vocation of every Christian, I felt conflicted. That is the reason why churches have activities every day of the week. The idea is to keep your attention so that you have less time to devote to the "things of the world." While there is a virtue in the intent, the approach is neither wise nor Biblical. However, some Christians would disagree with me. While you need fellowship and service, you do not need many activities that take away from personal development and time with family. Building and maintaining family and personal life is important. That is your first ministry, which must testify about - or demonstrate your attitude of service to God and others. I know of pastors and ministers who use their vacation time for hosting crusades, mission trips, and preaching in the churches of their friends while overseas They would then return from vacation reporting that they were tired. That is irresponsible and a lack of true leadership and self-management.

The Church emphasized works for God, not necessarily resting in God. And given that background, every time a believer said, "I am tired and need to rest," it was looked at negatively. However, we have a Biblical endorsement for rest and recreation. God rested on the seventh day after creation (Gen. 2:2-3) and in the commandments required a day of rest from the Children of Israel (Exod. 20:8-11). The humanity of Jesus Christ did not exempt Him from being tired. He rested because He was tired given the demands of the calling and the multitude who followed Him. As God, He did not need rest, but as the God-man He needed to rest, which provided us with an example of self-care in ministry.

> *But He was in the stern, asleep on a pillow. And they awoke Him and said to Him, "Teacher, do You not care that we are perishing?" (Mark 4:38).*

Now Jacob's well was there. Jesus therefore, being wearied from His journey, sat thus by the well. It was about the sixth hour (John 4:6).

Jesus also encourages us to rest.

Come to Me, all you who labor and are heavy-laden, and I will give you rest. Take My yoke upon you and learn from Me, for I am gentle and lowly in heart, and you will find rest for your souls. For My yoke is easy and My burden is light (Matt. 11:28-30).

And He said to them, "Come aside by yourselves to a deserted place and rest awhile."(Mark 6:31).

The rest represented in the texts was not only physical but spiritual. When we rest, our souls receive renewing and rejuvenation to complete other spiritual tasks just as our physical bodies also receive energy and vitality. Sometimes believers miss the importance of the dualism of rest and continue to exert themselves with both physical and spiritual work, forgetting that the work of Christ was already accomplished through the blood of Jesus on the cross. They also forget that it is the Holy Spirit who draws men to Christ. We must also understand that resting is not approving of laziness. It involves astute attention to self-care, facilitating the available flow of grace, and accomplishing the work of regeneration in our lives, through our submission to the Holy Spirit.

I will both lie down in peace, and sleep; For You alone, O Lord, make me to dwell in safety (Ps. 4:8).

Taking a break came with resistance from some believers and Christian family members who mistakenly felt that giving up some responsibilities meant that I was abandoning the ministry. Again, when I decided to obey God's instructions to leave Tobago, someone said I was running from Tobago, and questioned what will happen to family members who depended on me. Some asked, why did I need to make a move at that age when I was up for a promotion at work. They questioned my decision because the church where I was an assistant pastor had a vacancy for a pastor and I was the preferred candidate for the position. I knew what God said to me, and though the promotions were dreams come true and tempting, it was not the will of God for me at that season. I must confess that I struggled and battled a lot with indecision about some aspects of my journey. The most intense struggle came when I considered leaving some family members who depended on me behind. The truth is, I was broken and fatigued mentally, emotionally, spiritually, physically, and psychologically and could not give anymore.

I remember when I was saved and throughout my Christian walk, the Holy Spirit kept telling me, "Anne-Marie, I love you and there is no one else who can love you like Me, not even your family. I am jealous over you." Which always made me feel like His special child. At the time of conflict in making those decisions to put everything behind me and move on, I heard His voice again affirming His love for me. There was an additional word of comfort. I heard the Holy Spirit say, "You cannot love them more than me." I needed some healing. I resolved to say no and go through with the decision to save my life from an untimely dissolution, which seemed inevitable if I did not change some things. Yes, I said it. ***Untimely dissolution of my life.***

You would note that I mentioned the desire to please which was a constant character flaw in my life. I decided that it was either me or them. I was destroying my life from the inside out because I was also carrying hurt, pain, rejection, and grief from unresolved personal and ministerial experiences. There was also anxiety about some difficult family situations which affected my ability to sleep and rest. You see, the activities shrouded the issues and masked the reality of the damage the emotional and psychological turmoil contributed to my current health crisis.

Please keep in mind that I did not look like someone who was sick. There was no weight loss, or visible physical changes, except for my report on the diagnosis and complaints of being physically tired and exhausted. Given that disposition, I can understand some people's disbelief that I needed to take such drastic actions and give up my responsibilities. Some said nothing was wrong with me, or disbelieved my report and asked, "Are you sure something is wrong with you? You do not look like something is wrong with you." The medical professionals also said I looked okay, and it was difficult to tell if something was wrong. To date, I still do not know how I was supposed to look with that life-threatening diagnosis.

I was in a place I had never been in my human existence and Christian experience at age forty-six years. If I should describe that place it was a crossroads where existence met reality. That time was the opportune moment for being true to myself. Would it be thirsting for men's approval by saying yes, or valuing myself as a human being and agreeing to the need to pause and take care of myself? I said, "NO!" Against all odds I defied the opinion of men and pleased God and myself. I made the decision, no turning back now. I wrote my letters of resignation, leave of absence, sabbatical, and request for reduced duties because of the impending personal health crisis. Now it was time to develop a plan of action and wait to see the extent and effects of the outcome.

I had to reconcile that the path God was taking was unique to me because I had a unique design and purpose. I looked at other believers who I felt were not doing as much as I was doing for the kingdom, and did not have to face many fiery trials. Eventually, I changed my faulty thinking because the comparison was unjust and unrealistic. I submitted to the process of change, the shifting and reorganizing of my life, and the renewal of my focus on devotion to God, family, and vocation. I acquiesced to His call to self-love and self-care so that I could effectively give back from a place of love, knowledge, and understanding of God's purpose in this waiting season of my life. I could not tell the future outcome of the decision to submit, but I knew that I had nothing to lose. I found peace and confidence in God's Word. Just as God told Moses there was a place by Him, where he could experience His glory.

> *So it shall be, while My glory passes by, that I will put you in the cleft of the rock, and will cover you with My hand while I pass by (Exod. 33:22).*

I wanted to be in that place, and I found comfort in the Holy Spirit in that season, where His glory and grace covered me. A place where I could meet with him one on one, face to face. I told Him my fears, concerns, needs, and desires. In that place, I communed with Him who is my friend. I emptied my heart. A cry rose from the depths of my being. I needed help from God and there was no one else who could provide a solution at that time. My resolve was firm and secure in the love of God, that He knew what was best, and will direct my steps. Confidently yet filled with precariousness about the unchartered territories, I set my face towards the journey of healing and restoration, and I was not disappointed. My journey lay ahead of me but I also knew who would walk with me there.

CHAPTER 4

Defiant Fear or Determined Faith

No temptation has overtaken you except such as is common to man; but God is faithful, who will not allow you to be tempted beyond what you are able, but with the temptation will also make the way of escape, that you may be able to bear it.

(1 Cor. 10:13)

The phone call came. "Ms. James we are calling from the Social Welfare office of the Tobago Regional Health Authority to let you know that the hospital approved an application for the sum of TT $150,000 for your surgery at the St Clair Medical Facility." In disbelief, I processed what I just heard. I answered the young lady on the other end of the line and explained that I was currently in the United States for a consultation with a doctor and I will get back to them about my decision. I hung up the phone. I thought, God, how was it that approval came through quickly for something like that when I seemed unable to get a timely response for anything else in my life?

Let me explain what led up to that call. After my initial meeting with the nephrologist in January 2014, I was referred to a vascular surgeon in Trinidad since there was an absence of a qualified vascular surgeon resident in Tobago to mitigate my medical situation. I went to Trinidad in February 2014 and met with the doctor. He was baffled, intrigued, and stumped by my diagnosis, and asked many questions. He classified my diagnosis as a medical phenomenon and explained that any surgery would be intrusive and risky. He further recommended that I should think about the available options. He was more concerned about the presence of my reproductive problems, namely fibroids, and suggested that the fibroids would be an obstruction for any major surgery. He concluded that I should consider surgery for the removal of the fibroids first, before correcting the aneurysm. I was referred to an OBGYN at the same hospital and scheduled for monthly visits, which included CT scans, Magnetic Resonance Imaging (MRIs), Ultrasounds, and other relevant examinations. At that time, I became exhausted from the constant medical procedures and having dyes injected into my body.

On my first visit to the OBGYN at the Port of Spain General Hospital, the doctor informed me that he will not perform the surgery to remove fibroids unless they perform the surgery to correct the problem with the aneurysm first. What an irony! The hospital referred me to a private medical facility, West Shore Medical Centre, Port-of-Spain, Trinidad, for a second opinion. The doctor was curious and asked, "How did you discover this?" I told the same story all over again. After seeing my MRI results, he gave the same prognosis. It is risky, they can do it but.... and in any case, if something went wrong with the medical procedure there, they could not help.

On my second visit to the vascular surgeon who was also a professor at a medical university, I went into the room and saw at least seven medical students in their coats. It was the first time the students witnessed a patient with my diagnosis. They were curious and puzzled and asked some questions as he showed them the presence of the aneurysm in front of my kidneys on the X-rays. The doctor explained that he preferred not to perform a surgery like mine, since it meant taking out the right kidney, placing it on ice, removing the aneurysm, reconstructing the kidney, then placing it back into my body. He also explained that if anything went wrong with the surgery, I could lose my right kidney, but I could live with one kidney. However, he referred me to another doctor at another facility. That next medical facility was the St Clair Medical Centre, Port-of-Spain, Trinidad, one of the best private hospitals in the country. I was tired of the back and forth, traveling from Tobago to Trinidad, booking flights, taking taxis, visiting doctors both in Trinidad and Tobago, and depleting finances. It was an exhausting journey sometimes twice monthly, which spanned six months.

The doctor saw me in the first consultation and arranged for me to meet with two Venezuelan specialist vascular surgeons. They visited the hospital annually to perform procedures with critical patients for kidney or heart complications. I was scheduled for an invasive procedure where they made an incision from my groin area, inserted a tube, and sent dye into my system. The procedure called an angiogram helped to determine the level of functioning in my kidneys, and the size of the aneurysm. Before and after they engaged in the procedure, they asked many questions about how the primary care physician discovered the aneurysm, my symptoms, and my current level of discomfort. I was conscious because of the local anesthetic in my groin area, and they projected the images from the inserted camera on a screen. I was reminded of the seriousness of the diagnosis from observing the images.

I particularly remember the two doctors coming to my room in the recovery ward after the procedure as I waited before being discharged from the hospital. They expressed that it was their first time meeting a patient with that diagnosis, but also explained they did not know what my options were for treatment. As far as I knew, they were the experienced specialists who could give a possible intervention plan for my healing. Well, a bell went off again that I was in the presence of medical professionals who may not be able to give me an answer. I felt like a specimen, a guinea pig, an experiment with whom everyone was fascinated.

After my discharge, the medical assistant scheduled another appointment with the vascular surgeon within two weeks. He explained that when I meet with the doctor, he would give me the results of the angiogram and disclose what will be the next step in my treatment. When I returned to the follow-up appointment the doctor explained the results and what will be the possible procedure to remove the aneurysm. He explained the risks and I asked him if he had a previous patient with the same diagnosis as mine and whether he previously conducted a similar surgery. The doctor said yes. I looked at his face and eyes. I was not convinced that he was the specialist I would entrust my life to, and who knew what to do to correct the problem. I felt uncomfortable, as though I was an experiment given my unique diagnosis. He told me to go home and think about it and he would ask the administration to commence the process to take care of the financial aspects of the surgery with the Tobago Regional Health Authority.

I left the medical facility feeling burdened, and I carried that weight as I returned to Tobago. I had a difficult decision to make but the words I heard when I first received the diagnosis echoed in the back of my mind. "Do not let anyone touch you I will fix you for myself." Will my healing come directly from God or through surgery? What decision should I make? Do I say yes to the surgery, or should I wait? Do I take the risk, or should I just leave it alone, and whenever it was my time to leave this earth just accept my fate and go peacefully to meet the Lord?

After that time, some family members from the United States reached out and suggested that I should travel to the United States to consult with a doctor and receive a second opinion and I readily agreed. It was on that trip in July 2014 that I received the call that I could proceed with having the surgery at the St Clair Medical Facility in Trinidad.

On my return to Tobago from the medical doctors in Trinidad, I started to make plans for my funeral: the songs, the program, the people, the pictures. It became a pastime to mentally document who will receive my clothes, shoes, books, handbags, and jewelry. I started adding a beneficiary to my accounts and started drafting a will. Separating, disconnecting, and disassociating from people and things started happening without me realizing it. I spent less on things that seemed insignificant and focused on the journey before me. I struggled through those experiences of closure personally in my thoughts and actions, without confiding in anyone.

I saw the fear, pity, and empathy in the eyes of those with whom I shared the diagnosis, possible options for healing, and what I was experiencing. The helplessness I felt was real, but their look of help-lessness to do something to help me was also real and hurt deeply. The question was how much I could do to spare them from the fear and pain I saw in their eyes, while also remaining strong to get to a secure place so that the helplessness and fear will not destroy me. That is when I decided to have crazy determined faith and defy fear. The songs of faith, words of affirmation, and scriptures on life and living in that season began to consume my thoughts and mindset. My favourite scripture became my mantra.

For I know the thoughts that I think toward you, says the Lord, thoughts of peace and not of evil, to give you a future and a hope (Jer. 29:11).

Psalm 91 was a daily affirmation about God's ability to deliver me from the jaws of death and the bondage of sickness and disease. I spoke over my body healing and life and refused to complain but declared that:

I shall not die, but live, And declare the works of the Lord (Ps. 118:17).

I sang songs that uplifted my faith and pointed me in the direction of hope. Then my spirit began to lift. I felt hope, peace, and a blessed assurance that God knew why I was going through the challenge, and He had a plan. The Holy Spirit comforted me and reassured me that He will be with me and there was an end to what I was experiencing.

I remember when I shifted to a supervisory role in my job and no longer taught at the secondary school but continued visiting schools to monitor and supervise facilitators. Those journeys to the countryside were the best, especially at one time when I took a bus. I felt relaxed because of the natural air and the scenery. Observing the vegetation, the waves rolling on the shores, and sometimes the breeze blowing on my face was a blessing. I experienced peace and a feeling of being one with nature and God, and I treasured those times. My faith expanded, and my passion for God increased with quiet reassurance.

For thus says the Lord God, the Holy One of Israel: n returning and rest you shall be saved; In quietness and confidence shall be your strength (Isaiah 30:15)

I was determined that what does not break me will make me stronger and I had no intention of breaking. I knew it was time to grow in my faith walk since our faith pleases God and creates a gateway for Him to act on our behalf.

> *But without faith, it is impossible to please Him, for he*
> *who comes to God must believe that He is, and that He is*
> *a rewarder of those who diligently seek Him (Heb. 11:6)*

How can a believer increase their faith? Only through accessing the truth of the Scriptures and meditating on the promises of God.

> *So then faith comes by hearing, and hearing by the word*
> *of God (Rom. 10:17).*

Just in case it may seem that I made this journey from fear to faith seem easy I must confess it was not. I had to constantly live in the realm of victory rather than defeat, even when I did not feel like it. You see, it may have been easier if I was told by the doctors that there was a cure through medication, or surgery can correct the defect, or rest would heal my body for certainty, but there was nothing to go on. I said to myself, "Just live with the uncertainty Anne-Marie." The statement required a crazy faith that will not let up no matter how I felt. Remember I did not feel sick during that time, there were no incessant symptoms. Neither were there any visible physical signs that something was wrong. The only symptoms were periodical tiredness and slight discomfort in my lower back. When I changed my diet, I lost some weight and started to look fit. Some people commented that my exterior posturing was peaceful. That disposition came only from resting in the abiding peace of God.

… and the peace of God, which surpasses all understanding, will guard your hearts and minds through Christ Jesus (Phil. 4:7).

Dear reader when you face a crisis that wants to destroy your very being, there must be a determination to stand strong even though you feel like crumbling. Stand strong to the end. You must be like Esther saying, "If I perish, I perish but I am going to see the King." (Esther 4:16). It takes a reckless faith to go against an army with the jaw-bone of a donkey, just like Samson did (Judges 15:15-16), or to face a giant with a slingshot and some stones, like David (1 Sam. 17:1-58). Those Biblical heroes did not faint in the face of insurmountable obstacles against their destiny or the destiny of the people and nation they represented. Rather they defied all opposition and trusted God to make a way in situations that defied natural circumstances. They invited the divine initiator of all great things to supernaturally intervene in earthly affairs through them as humble vessels. The divine hand changed the course of negative earthly events which confronted them. Only God can do that, and I knew beyond the shadow of a doubt that I needed that determined faith.

Reaching out, I grasped the promises of God for me. I adhered to earlier prophetic utterances received during my early Christian experience and determined that my purpose on earth was incomplete and there was so much more to do. I spoke to myself that God did not expect my service to Him and others in the Kingdom to end that way. I chose to allow this temporary period of suffering to reflect God's ability to keep all that I committed to Him when I first said yes to serving Him. I wanted all to see that the God I served was real and faithful. To this day I question how I survived that stormy season. I marvel at the discovery that I had an inner strength that I did not know of until faced with the medical crisis. I believe that anyone can develop that resilience and it is within all humanity. However, some people can tap into it when necessary and others are afraid or lack the support or emotional intelligence to discover an aspect of themselves, they never knew existed. I dare you to take a leap of faith today. Wherever you are, whatever you are facing, there is a way of escape and courage lies within you. Trust God take His hand and He will fix it for you.

CHAPTER 5

Carrying the Cross While Wearing the Crown

And he said, "Abba, Father, all things are possible for You. Take this cup away from Me; nevertheless, not what I will, but what you will.

(Mark 14:36)

I t was August 2014 and I had just left the Methodist hospital in Brooklyn, New York, after my first visit with the vascular surgeon. As I walked to the train station with one of my cousins, I reflected on the last words the doctor shared with me after I asked him what I should do about my diagnosis and if I could start exercising. He said, "Anne-Marie go home, enjoy your life and have fun." As I recalled his words and the tears streamed down my face, I resolved that somehow, I would need to find a way to live through this storm and function as normal as possible, but I must enjoy my life because I was not sure what would happen.

That was the second time in my life that my stance about who I am, and how I lived my life, experienced a significant metamorphosis. I changed to being a woman on a mission because of the advice of the doctor and the awareness of the uncertainty of my health. The mission included being the best me with the limited options and time available to make a difference in the lives of others. This time around, the dynamics were different, the focus was less directed at serving but on self-development; being rather than doing. Isn't it amazing that God will meet us anywhere and when He shows up it illuminates the darkness and despair and brings comfort and peace? God meets us and it creates an avalanche of clarity when fear encounters faith and calling, and God intersects our desires with His will.

DIVINITY MEETING HUMANITY

Reflecting on the life and ministry of Jesus Christ, I realized that he conducted his ministry on earth with the impending reality of the ultimate sacrifice before Him. To redeem the sins of mankind. He framed every act of ministry against the background of that sacrifice and declared:

> "… *My food is to do the will of Him who sent Me, and to finish His work"(John 4:34).*

> *For even the Son of Man did not come to be served, but to serve, and to give His life a ransom for many (Mark 10:45).*

Behold, we are going up to Jerusalem, and the Son of Man
will be betrayed to the chief priests and the scribes and they
will condemn Him to death (Matt. 20:18-19).

Every act of service and teaching was couched against the background of the cross. Jesus Christ knew that his obeisance to God and his purpose required certainty in objectivity, thinking, and action. Humility and grace helped him navigate the difficult seasons of ministry when he came face to face with the inevitability of his earthly mission. He wore the crown while carrying his cross. He was the sacrificial lamb assigned to lay down his life for humanity's sins but also the King of the heavenly kingdom.

…but made himself of no reputation, taking the form of a
bondservant, and coming in the likeness of men (Phil. 2:7).

Observe Jesus Christ as he focused on ministry and walked on the road to Calvary with the view of impending death on the cross before him. He knew what he came to earth to accomplish but did it with a sense of urgency, devotion, and passion, knowing that his purpose was greater than the pain. All the anticipation of his final sojourn on earth came to a place of reckoning in the garden of Gethsemane as he bared himself in prayer and his humanity reflected the conflict of wills. He took the cross as the King of the Kingdom and carried it. Carrying the cross did not change who he was, he was still king, saviour, and Lord, but he also bled, suffered, and died. Divinity met humanity at a place of grace. Completing his mission on the earth stayed at the forefront until it was complete, and He cried out, **"It is finished!"**

So when Jesus had received the sour wine, He said, "It is finished!" And bowing His head, He gave up His Spirit (John 19:30).

THE CROSS AND THE CROWN

God calls all believers and those who would trust Him to **wear their crowns while carrying their cross.** God positioned called-out ones as **royal priesthood, heir and joint-heirs, and peculiar people** (Rom. 8:17; I Peter 2:9). In that position, we are qualified to wear the crown, but with the crown comes responsibility and with responsibility, there are obstacles and trials.

Yes, and all who desire to live godly in Christ Jesus will suffer persecution (2 Tim. 3:12).

While Jesus called all believers to carry their cross and serve him, there is a greater demand for those who occupy the forefront in the ministerial offices. The pastors, teachers, apostles, prophets, and evangelists are the overseer ministers given to the church to equip the saints and prepare them for ministry to the body of Christ (Eph. 4:11). Those positions demand abiding peace and grace even when struggling with personal trials and conflicting situations. Sometimes ministers continue to serve while carrying the weight of personal fears, family challenges, financial difficulties, sinful struggles, shame, guilt, abandonment, unresolved feelings of rejection, and unrealistic expectations. They obeyed the calling to wear the crown not recognizing that they would simultaneously need to carry their cross.

Then He said to them all, "If anyone desires to come after Me, let him deny himself, and take up his cross daily, and follow me (Luke 9:23).

There are those moments when the desire to do God's will meets the desire to say my body, mind, and spirit cannot endure the persecution and the expectations to look good in the eyes of others. You desire to always represent God from a place where you do not expose your vulnerabilities because your followers, colleagues, and friends will perceive you as a weak person. You sometimes wonder who has your back and the external fervor does not match the internal struggles. The seeming appearance of a following, growth, and charisma, mask the reality of what is happening behind the scenes. In those moments you realize that you have an option, whether to continue on a path that you know will undoubtedly lead to your demise or to cry out **"I NEED HELP!"** It takes a special grace, and humility to ask for help, the same that is needed to wear the crown and carry the cross. Each person must know when they can no longer do it alone. No one can do that for you, but you. I knew my moment came when I needed help to carry the cross while wearing my crown. **Yes, my crown!** God called me to a purpose, and I was the only one who could wear that crown and carry that cross. You see everyone has their crown and their cross. Only you and God know the weight of your crown and the value of carrying it.

For whoever desires to save his life will lose it, but whoever loses his life for My sake will save it (Luke 9:24).

I carried personal crosses of childhood family dysfunction, rejection, failure, sickness, condemnation, false expectations, unfulfilled goals, and broken relationships. This was also exacerbated because

I was a single woman in ministry and felt that I did not receive the same support that I anticipated because of unrealistic expectations. The support available to men was more visible because of some stereotypes which exist about women in ministry. Though there seemed to be visible acceptance, at that time there were some microaggressions that existed then and currently exist in some organizations about the extent to which a woman can contribute to the ministry. Sometimes those misconceptions can relegate women to traditional roles.

After understanding my purpose and calling I learned to trust my calling to the one who called me to the ministry for His purpose. That journey required my commitment and a willingness to surrender those insecurities to God and continue to say yes, knowing that I was enough, even when I felt the rejection. I am also grateful that I had some Godly women, ministerial mentors, and coaches, who stood in the gap for and with me. I also had some Godly men who supported, encouraged, and motivated me to fulfill my calling. However, the questions, suspicions, and being judged for not having a husband were crosses I carried. The emotional turmoil no doubt affected my health and could have resulted in a life-threatening diagnosis. I had to learn how to walk through this season of pain with the right attitude and not lose the true essence of who I was, what God wanted me to be, and the lessons He wanted me to learn. I learned how to carry my cross while wearing the crown by maintaining the right attitude instead of blaming and continuing to question God. Having a firm grip on the intentionality of mission, purposeful living, and ministry was the key to my strength to carry my cross.

There was one significant change that I noticed in my attitude. Before I knew the diagnosis, I would feel tired and breathless when preaching so I took some time off preaching, and I generally became quiet and did not speak much. Although one can consider me a reserved and introverted person, I always had an opinion and would be vocal in meetings or open forums, because I believed in advocacy for change and the rights of individuals. However, I listened more and contributed less to calm my spirit. My persona took on a view of the fragility of human life and the unpredictability of life events. I empathized more with the misfortune of others and embraced the journey of change by observing the suffering of others during the hospital visits while talking with other patients and meeting with my doctors. I also learned how to reach out and ask for help from others while building significant supportive relationships.

HELP TO CARRY THE CROSS

While Jesus Christ walked the road to Golgotha with the cross on his back, there was a moment when the soldiers realized the cross became too heavy (Matthew 27:32). There will always be a point in the journey when your cross becomes heavy, and you need someone to come alongside you and help you carry your cross. The soldiers took Jesus' cross and gave it to a bystander (Simon the Cyrene), who carried it for the rest of the journey to Golgotha hill: although unwillingly since the soldiers forced him to carry it (Matt.27:32-33). When the entourage got to Golgotha Jesus resumed his role of carrying the cross and they eventually nailed him to that cross. This action I believe symbolized that we who receive him as King and Lord of our lives, do not have to carry our cross alone. Additionally, there are some crosses you need to let go of because the vicarious and efficacious sacrifice Jesus accomplished was enough to take care of your sins, and the blood that was shed for you has washed you clean. The willingness to reach out and accept help is the difference between completing your journey or sabotaging your destiny.

On his earthly journey, Jesus Christ surrounded himself with twelve disciples (Luke 6:12-16), who accompanied him on his earthly mission. Within that group, he had an inner circle who understood him in a way that the other disciples did not (Luke 5:4-11). Peter, James, and John stood with him during some of the significant experiences in his ministry and carried a zeal and care for the mission (Matt. 26:36-38; Mark 9:2-3; Luke 8:49-56). Jesus knew that they would struggle to stand with him during the final days of carrying the cross and his death. He also knew they would be among those apostles who will carry the gospel throughout the nations after his resurrection and the birth of the church. He knew the same people he fed the loaves of bread and fishes would also be the ones who would yell, **"Crucify Him!"** He needed a small group who would stand with him when that time came, although they did not. As you carry your cross, God would bring you alongside people who would hold up your hand. It will be just as Aaron and Hur held up the hand of Moses when he became tired after holding up his hand with the rod so that the Israelites would win the battle against the Amalekites (Exod. 17:12). You need people around you to figuratively hold up your hands. To stand with you and support you on your journey to healing and restoration when no one else will stand with you or believe in you.

Your mission and purpose are always attached to people, and because of that, God would use people who can stand with you in those moments when it is most difficult to pursue the goals of your purpose. I could not tell my family members all that was happening but I gave them enough information so they would not worry too much. It did not help much because I saw the concerns, fears, and pain on their faces whenever I spoke about the diagnosis. Therefore, I chose some close friends and associates to confide in. They were the ones who accompanied me to the doctor and held my hand when I felt weary. Now everyone can rejoice when they see what the Lord has done, by causing the mountain of sickness and disease in my life to crumble and fall.

The lesson here is that you cannot expect anyone to understand your journey and carry your cross, they can help you, but you alone can carry it because there is a cross for everyone. Eventually, your sacrifices will go on that cross, but you alone will not reap the benefits of that sacrifice. Even on the cross until death, Jesus wore the crown and continued to fulfill his mission by offering pardon to the thieves. The fact that you may be carrying the cross does not negate the calling of God on your life. The calling remains. What changes is your ability to remain faithful and lean into the grace of God. Paul knew that only too well as he spoke about the thorns in the flesh. He cried to God earnestly and continuously to remove it, but God instead provided grace to endure. Paul decided to focus on the mission and allow God to accomplish His will through his life and suffering and said:

> *And lest I should be exalted above measure by the abundance of the revelations, a thorn in the flesh was given to me, a messenger of Satan to buffet [beat] me, lest I be exalted above measure. Concerning this, I pleaded with the Lord three times that it might depart from me. And He said to me, "My grace is sufficient for you, for My strength is made perfect in weakness." Therefore most gladly I will rather boast in my infirmities, that the power of Christ may rest upon me (2 Cor. 12:7-9).*

We cannot fathom the crosses we will encounter and what God will allow into our lives. We cannot predict how God will respond in the vicissitudes of life, but we know He promised to be with us and He will never leave us (Heb. 13:5). While I continued the journey, I reaffirmed the promises of God and remembered His promises made to me while I was a teenager, starting ministerial training, entering full-time ministry, and at that moment when I needed Him more than before.

I walked away from the doctor's office to my cousin's residence in New York in August 2014 with a wave of peace and grace, knowing that God was with me. My cousin advised me that I should trust God and obey the doctor's instructions. I got on that plane back to Tobago at the end of August 2014 with a fresh outlook on life and the cross I carried. Yes, I will carry my cross, but it was also time to fully wear my crown without fear and condemnation. Some people say to me you are strong. Yes, I am, but only because I learned how to appropriate the measure of grace God deposited in my life. You must also do the same while carrying your crown. I had to preach to myself, and I even read the first book I authored in 2009 *The Seasons of Your Life* to encourage myself in the Lord.

Do you remember David in 1 Samuel 30 when the armies of the Amalekites derailed the camp of Judah while they were in Ziklag? The Amalekites also burned their city and took their wives, sons, and daughters captive. The men blamed David for what happened and wanted to stone him. David's posturing included the following:

- ✦ *He encouraged himself in the Lord*
- ✦ *He inquired of the Lord*
- ✦ *He searched the mind of God for instructions*
- ✦ *He followed the instructions of the Lord*

There must always be a posture of humility to enquire about the mind and heart of God in any matter. After that, we must wait for His response and trust His directives until He fulfills His plans. Any impulsive decision will only lead to regret and unforeseen consequences. **Carry your cross but remember who you are, and whose you are. YOU ARE ROYALTY!**

CHAPTER 6

New Perspectives Towards Purpose

Then the Lord answered me and said: "Write the vision, and make it plain on tablets, that he may run who reads it."

(Hab. 2:2)

When I got on that plane at John F Kennedy (JFK) international airport in New York City and headed back to the beautiful Caribbean island of Tobago in August 2014, I was not the same person who entered the United States a month before. Thoughts, feelings, and attitudes began to shift towards a different perspective of what I was experiencing physically. If this diagnosis had no cure and I could not do surgery because it was risky, then my life's existence is unpredictable, and this was something I had to live with. ***I had to make some decisions.***

As I mentioned before, I made some changes to my diet, vocation, and family time, and also focused on what brought me joy. At that moment, what mattered most was not material possessions or accomplishments, but living meaningfully every day with family and the people who were closest to me. Without the involvement in activities, my relationship with Jesus took on a new meaning of waiting, reflecting, and leaning into what he wanted and where he was leading. I wanted to please him, I inquired of him with every decision. I also recommitted to becoming attuned to my body and soul. Simultaneously, I was doing exactly as the doctor said, enjoying life, taking care of myself, and having fun.

Emotionally, I was no longer in turmoil and confusion. I felt peace, grace, compassion, and humility in my journey. Like any other person who experienced a crisis, I knew pain, fear, remorse, uncertainty, grief, and discomfort; just like the people, I ministered to for the past twenty years. I was one with them and touched by their struggles, although mine was different from theirs. Now I understood and felt an affinity with their pain. When previously I could only empathize, **now I knew it!**

The second reality check came when I was on the plane back to Tobago after my second trip to the vascular surgeon in January of 2015. I had to make a second trip because the doctor required me to schedule a follow-up appointment every six months to observe any changes with the aneurysm. On that visit, the doctor gave me the same advice. There were no changes, take care of my health and do what was needed to enjoy my life. He reaffirmed that they could not recommend surgery but requested that I return in six months.

The Lord spoke to me. I heard the words in my spirit. "Anne-Marie you must prepare to leave Tobago. I will be shifting you." I was startled and began to internally reason with what I just heard. What! Now? Lord, you cannot be serious! Move to the United States? At the time when I wanted to move to the United States, you did not allow it and now you want me to move when I do not want to move. I was headed for promotion at work, and possibly a new leadership position as a Pastor. Ok then.

When I stepped from the plane as it touched down in Tobago, I felt like a new woman with an understanding that I carried a destiny, dream, and goal exceeding my capability and capacity. There was renewed hope because of that word from the Holy Spirit, but also concern about how it will happen.

I continued visiting the doctors in Tobago for my scheduled appointments, however, the visits ended when they realized my diagnosis was in stasis and there was nothing they could do. I reasoned, why should I continue seeing the doctors if the results were the same? I set my heart to focus on preparation to obey God and leave Tobago when it was God's appointed time. I was back to Anne-Marie mode (independent and strategic) and making plans for my life concerning what I thought it should look like.

The third revelation from God came when I heard the Holy Spirit speaking again, "Anne-Marie there is a place in the ministry you need to go for the next step of the journey, and you will not advance anymore without a husband. You need a husband!" Huh! What? I thought. I was getting to a comfortable place being single and all the intimate relationships I had up to that point did not work out. I was satisfied at my age that I could remain single and continue doing ministry. At least that is what I thought, but God had a different plan. I did not believe my feelings were wrong, but it was not aligned with God's will for my life at that time.

I am reminded of Mary, the mother of Jesus after the angels visited her and said she would be the mother of the promised Messiah. Mary questioned them about the plausibility of the revelation and her suitability for the role. With her finite understanding, she struggled to envision an infinite declaration.

Then Mary said to the angel, "How can this be, …?
(Luke 1:34).

51

After the angel responded and explained what will happen, Mary's concluding position was to ponder on what she heard and maintain a position of secrecy, until the time for the manifestation of the spoken word.

> *But Mary kept all these things and pondered them in her heart (Luke 2:19).*

Like Mary, I pondered the word of God and asked Him for clarification and direction on what He required me to do at that time. I did not have any idea how to make the first move. I knew some ministers in the United States where I could continue in Ministry; but will they receive me? The questions were endless. Some mitigating circumstances made a move seem impossible at that moment. My first thought was where will I go, and at my age… I was forty-seven and believed that I should be settling. In fact, my life was settling, promotion, advancement in ministry, and pursuing further education so that I would be more positioned financially to accomplish career and ministerial goals. I had no children or husband so there were no limitations on what I could do. **Then *bam!* Time to move!** My life took unpredictable turns, and one would think that I should have been accustomed to those turns at that time, but I was caught off guard. What I thought was the end was the beginning of a new adventure that eventually blew my mind. Given the uncertainty of how to proceed with the directive from God, I had to keep quiet until I knew what to do.

The next concern I had was my family. What will happen to the family members that I took care of, and what will happen with other family commitments? That is when I tried to reorganize God's directive. I concluded that I would go to study and return to Tobago after two years because by that time my body would heal and I could continue with my ministerial and vocational pursuits. I gradually began to craft a plan and shared it with those in my significant relationships, like family and employers. My employers decided that I would be appointed to the position of program director after I resumed my two-year hiatus in the United States. My family believed I would return after two years, and that reassurance gave them some comfort. It appeared the plan was all set and it seemed like a good plan, or so I thought. To tell you a bit about the significance of planning. I was always a planner. Every year I had a diary and planner to schedule my meetings and set goals for the year. Most of the time, I stuck with my plans with some flexibility for interruptions, but for the most part, I stuck to the plans. Knowing that the current plans kept changing and nothing was working out the way I thought, was disconcerting for me. However, with the medical diagnosis, God shook every plan and shattered it to the very core. We cannot predict the mind of God and determine how He would intervene in the circumstances of our lives. His word declares:

> *For My thoughts are not your thoughts, Nor are your ways*
> *My ways, says the Lord (Isa. 55:8).*

I was making a plan that was not aligned with the instructions and the purposes of God but did not know that at the time. The only recourse was to fall in alignment with the purposes of God. God is the one who turns our hearts and orders our steps when we give them to Him.

> *There are many plans in a man's heart, Nevertheless the*
> *Lord's counsel--that will stand (Prov. 19:21).*

We must remember that we cannot take away control from God after we surrender our lives to Him but must attune to His directive so that we do not walk in disobedience. We cannot board an airplane, and after sitting when the plane left for its assigned destination, go to the cockpit, and ask the pilot to allow us to fly the plane in any direction when we know we are not qualified for the job. The pilot possesses the qualifications, approvals, and manifests for the flight. As it is in the natural so too is the lesson in the spiritual. God is our pilot, He possesses the blueprints of our existence, and He is leading our lives on this journey. We relinquished our role in directing the purposes of our lives when we said yes to Him at that moment of salvation. If we want Him to continue the work of regeneration in our spiritual journey, we must allow Him to take the wheel of our lives.

NEW PLACES NEW TERRITORIES

The Holy Spirit began to work on my thinking to create new places and new territories. Listen, when God gives us a word, He expects movement, He expects a response that says, Yes Lord speak! He expects obedience. I wanted to obey, I wanted to do His will I wanted to be in His plan, and I finally said yes, without the details. We do not need all the details because if God should expose the full trajectory of our lives, we cannot handle the contents. The Christian walk is one of faith and includes trusting God with every step of our journey.

One night, during that time of preparation and waiting, I had a dream about threading a needle, which was an insightful revelation about understanding my journey. The eye of the needle was small, and I tried to thread the needle many times but was unsuccessful. There were other events in the dream but when I woke up the event of attempting to thread the needle is what I remembered the most.

The frustration I felt in the dream made me realize that my current experience was significant. I asked God to reveal what the dream meant, and He gave the revelation. He responded that He wanted to fine-tune my vision and give me a clear view of what He was about to do. He wanted me to understand that it was connected to my current experiences, but I must see it through the eyes of the supernatural. It was at that time that I recognized my thinking and response changed. Before then, I saw the circumstances surrounding my health as negative, but His word gave me a different perspective and I heeded His word and the revelation through the lens of His Spirit. I knew that I needed Him now more than ever and could not go through this journey without the Holy Spirit.

My new perspective took on a new focus on accessing God's ability, strength, grace, and vision for my life. When God calls us to newness there must be a shift in our thinking and response. This action is predictable and should reflect the change that occurred. Paul clearly outlined the possibilities and boundaries of the renewed mindset. A renewed mindset moves from a place of not knowing to a place of illumination.

> *And do not be conformed to this world, but be transformed by the renewing of your mind, that you may prove what is that good and acceptable and perfect will of God (Rom. 12:2).*

It is only when we allow a change in our thinking and we start assessing the situations in our lives from a renewed mind (a mind cleansed by the redemptive work of the blood of Jesus Christ), that we can connect with the mind of Jesus Christ. Renewal is the work of the Holy Spirit.

> *... and be renewed in the spirit of your mind (Eph. 4:23).*

The Apostle Paul encouraged believers to have the mind of Christ.

> *Let this mind be in you which was also in Christ Jesus…*
> *(Phil. 2:5).*

When the change in our thinking happens then we can know what the will of God is, His heart toward us, and what He requires of us in everyday life events.

The brain possesses the capacity to change faulty thinking. The amygdala is in the frontal part of the brain called the limbic system, and processes and facilitates change. The limbic system provides cognitive and emotional support. Brain circuitry is the term used to identify the collection of areas of the brain that organizes themselves together to accomplish brain function. The brain is referred to as elastic, also defined as brain plasticity. The brain's plasticity provides it with the ability to change and redefine itself according to our experiences and focus on what is important at the moment. It is a self-regulating function of re-wiring itself through patterns of emotions, drives, planning, organizing, and behaviors.[12]

When Paul speaks of changing our minds, it is said with the understanding that our brains can rewire wrong thinking which does not serve to accomplish the will of God in our lives. That change in thinking starts with a change of heart. The heart is the core of one's being and operates through our soulish realm which initiates the desires of the mind, will, and emotions. Those responses to our thoughts and inclinations from the heart reflect who we are. Solomon said we are what we think in our hearts.

> *For as he thinks in his heart, so is he… (Prov. 23:7).*

God wants us to submit to the process of changing our faulty thinking by believing His word about who we are through Christ. It is not only enough to have a change in thinking, but a responsive change in action must accompany the change in thinking. The scripture in Philippians 2:5 mentioned above reflects Christ's willingness to sacrifice self, and repudiate self-preservation, as he did the will of his Father. It speaks to humility and grace in the face of humiliation. It is an unselfish disregard to please self in the face of impending disgrace before the eyes of men. The incarnation of Jesus Christ reflected in the verse is one of the fundamental examples and dogmas of Christian service and devotion. A regenerated spirit visualizes events, experiences, and activities through a regenerated heart. Our thoughts, behaviors, and motives must reflect those which Christ possessed. It is not selfish to do what God requires when others will not or try to dissuade us from being obedient to God, despite the consequences.

NEW PERSPECTIVE FOR NEW TERRITORIES

I am sure you will agree with me that we love the cushion of the familiar space. Do you know the saying; "…an old broom knows the corners." Eventually, the old broom will lose its' bristles and become useless. That comfort zone of constancy must sometimes yield to change. At the time when God spoke to me about leaving Tobago, I felt that it was a matter of life or death. My body, soul, and spirit could no longer thrive on the island. I felt like it was sucking the life out of me: emotionally suffocated, spiritually stagnated, vocationally unchallenged, financially bankrupt. I wanted more. I had no more to give and needed a change but did not realize how much I needed it until God spoke. You see some of us get accustomed to the norms of our current and familiar system that we become blinded to the effects it has on us. Change awaits until that critical moment when something happens and then God gets our attention. Sometimes God will use any crisis to get your attention. Is He trying to get your attention? ***God had my attention!***

I felt like Abraham (who carried the name Abram before God called him) when God uprooted him from the land of Ur in the Chaldeans and told him to pack up, take his family, get out and travel to an unknown place; *the promised land.*

> *Now the Lord had said to Abram, "Get out of your country, from your family and from your father's house, to a land that I will show you"(Gen. 12:1).*

God's intention is always to lead us into His promised place, a place of peace where His presence dwells. Our pre-ordained destiny place that He created and only He, the omnipotent one, knows. However, we must be willing and obedient to go when He asks us to and come when He calls us to Himself. We must always acquiesce to His prerogative since it will auger well for our Christian walk and general well-being. God's commands are not grievous:

> *For this is the love of God, that we keep His commandments. And his commandments are not burdensome (1 John 5:3).*

We cannot believe or accept that His intention is harmful since He always leads us into green pastures. It may not seem that way initially when He calls us because of the uncertainty of the journey, and that is why He asks us to trust Him with our lives so that we will reap the rewards of obedience. **I had to believe that the God I served for more than thirty years of my existence, the one who saved me at age thirteen years, was the same God who will bring me through this experience.** I knew He always led me into unchartered territories and rough waters and brought me out, and if He said move, I had to move. Therefore, while relocation was the furthest decision from my mind, I prepared my heart to do what He asked. I started in that season of pain and uncertainty to remember my Christian walk and journey in service to Him and others. I reminisced about being a teenager when I started teaching Sunday School in my village at age thirteen after the teacher did not show up for classes one day. I was not baptized yet, and I continued teaching Sunday school for years into my early forties. I remembered the times of fasting and prayer, camps, retreats, and deeper life sessions. I thought about ministry in foreign places: Africa, England, the United States, and the Caribbean Islands. Then I remembered the miracles He accomplished in my life. The opened doors I thought could never open. His protection when I walked through dangerous valleys. The time when the cares of this world tried to consume me.

I asked God to remember the crusades, community work, unselfish service, and labor of love. Why did I ask Him to remember? Not that God did not remember, but it was my way of saying to Him, "Lord you brought me this far, I trusted you then, and I am trusting you now to take care of me." You see, when the children of Israel journeyed to the promised land, every time God did a miracle and supernaturally intervened in their affairs to provide for and protect them, they erected stones of remembrance (Josh. 4:1-24) or built altars from stones (Exod. 15:17). These were symbolic of their faith and thankfulness for God's intervention in battles they could not fight without Him. He supernaturally orchestrated a mighty deliverance in situations that seemed naturally insurmountable.

When I attended primary school, my class teacher planned an outing for the class. She took us to a museum with artifacts from the early settlers on the island of Tobago. At the museum, we saw many symbolic representations that told us the Carib and Arawak tribes occupied the island before my fore parents' generations from African slaves. As we looked in awe at the artifacts, each had the writings of what they represented, and the guide told the story of their origins. It was a fascinating experience I never forgot. It told a story of previous life and events, which paved the way for our progress. They served as a point of reference, demonstrating where we came from, and the changes made along the way.

My gesture of calling to memory past events was signalling God's promises and a reminder of His goodness and faithfulness. It reflected that in this new journey I chose to trust Him every step of the way because I knew His plan was best and will come to fruition.

> *The Lord of hosts has sworn, saying, "Surely, as I have thought, so it shall come to pass, and as I have purposed, so it shall stand" (Isa. 14:24).*

There is something else we must understand concerning any decision to obey. I knew that my decision to obey God was also laying a foundation and creating stones of remembrance for the next generation in my lineage, both physically and spiritually. This new perspective was not only about me but it was also linked to creating and leaving a legacy for others. When Joseph, through a series of unfortunate events orchestrated by his jealous brothers, but divinely appointed by God became king in Egypt, he decided to forgive his brothers. He knew that his current position did not rely on their actions but God's providence.

> *But now, do not, therefore, be grieved or angry with yourselves because you sold me here; for God sent me before you to preserve life… And God sent me before you*

> *to preserve a posterity for you in the earth, and to save*
> *your lives by a great deliverance (Gen. 45:5-7).*

His reassuring words to them inform us that he had the correct perspective of who he was and his purpose as an instrument in God's hands. He continued to speak to them and give them hope for the restoration of their relationship. God was also interested in preserving for Himself a godly heritage.

> *But as for you, you meant evil against me; but God meant*
> *it for good, in order to bring it about as it is this day, to*
> *save many people alive. Now therefore, do not be afraid; I*
> *will provide for you and your little ones. And he comforted*
> *them and spoke kindly to them (Gen. 50:20-21).*

In the book of Judges, after Joshua died, it is recorded that the current generation of Israelites did not seek after God. Only one generation survived and went with Joshua to the promised land. Those who knew of God's mighty acts did not preserve the remembrance of His deeds or transfer them to the succeeding generations. The result was a loss of the desire to worship the true and living God.

> *When all that generation had been gathered to their*
> *fathers, another generation arose after them who did not*
> *know the Lord nor the work which He had done for Israel*
> *(Judges 2:10).*

Obedience is a key factor in transferring blessings to the next generation (Lev. 26:3-10; Deut. 28:1-2; 30:2, 9-10; I Sam. 15:22). Obedience to God is not a choice for the person who follows Christ, but rather it is a prerequisite in God's economy of returns.

*If you are willing and obedient, You shall eat the good of
the land (Isa. 1:19).*

My obedience and willingness to do what God said had the potential to transfer to other generations in my family, since I represented a strong influence and functioned as an example and mentor for my nieces and nephews. My obedience was centered on maintaining a generational perspective.

When love calls you home and you obey, there will be a restoration of relationships and a responsive generational impact! Never forget that.

A decision to walk with God is a decision to affect change not only in our lives but in the lives of others, to preserve a heritage. As I changed my perspective, I saw the good, not wholly, but in part. Step by step it kept unfolding as God directed. It was not that my spirit did not continue to war sometimes about the decision, but I found a place of peace and reassurance when I focused on the promises and sovereignty of God.

THE FLIGHT

To fly
Perchance to elude this seeming morass
Or is it to escape the thoughts within
Which puts one's mind in grim apprehension
So that all reality is but a dream

To fly
Maybe I cannot face this fear on my own
Or is it the thought of being alone
Where will meets choice but cannot choose
Yet knowing that only one path I can tread
And there's nothing to lose

To fly
Seeking worlds unknown only dreamt of
Knowing that my life here is a small dot
Significant though small
I know the worth of it is my call

I fly
Reaching for what is my destiny
Aiming to please Him the one who created me
Not searching anymore but reaching
Not running anymore but leaning
On the one who is my King and maker of my destiny
Not dreaming but living
With Him, I take my flight

Anne-Marie James-Henry© 2015

CHAPTER 7

Navigating New Pathways to Purpose

The steps of a good man are ordered by the Lord, And He delights in His way. Though he falls, he shall not be utterly cast down; For the Lord upholds him with His hand.

(Ps. 37:23-24)

Purpose always causes movement forward. A lack of purpose produces stagnation. Even though I knew what God said to me, I was not clear about how and why. If you are like me and ask questions or are a critical thinker, you know sometimes it can be a hindrance in your spiritual walk if you are unwilling to just follow God's instructions. He may show us the ending but not the in-between of the journey. I believe that action is wisdom and sovereignty in operation because if God showed some of us the in-between, we would not start on our journey by faith. Since the Christian walk is one of faith, we must trust God because it would help us develop spiritual muscles. Faith is the catalyst for spiritual growth. It is like water and sunlight. A plant needs sunlight for growth and nourishment. If you feed it daily, it will blossom, and if you starve it the plant will die. Therefore, we must trust Him with every step of our journey. That trust grows by feeding our spirits the truth of God's Word.

THE ARCHER AND THE ARROW

While contemplating this new journey and migration, I attended an annual women's conference, and the guest speaker was a visiting apostle, a well-respected man of God, who authored several books, is well travelled and the overseer of many congregations. The foreword of my book was written by the Apostle, whom I knew for several years, though not personally. At the conference, there was an awesome manifestation of the power of God and he ministered to me and declared, through the word of wisdom, the change that I was experiencing. I received confirmation about writing and other words of positive declaration over my life. After the meeting, the apostle asked to speak with me. I shared some of what I was experiencing and the uncertainty about my new course in life. I told him I felt that my life was having a setback and then he told me something so profound that it remained with me. He said, "When an arrow is about to be launched and it is placed in a bow. You usually pull it back before you can release and launch it." He said, "You are not being delayed, God is just allowing a break by pulling you back so that when the time is right, He will launch you forth in a mighty and unfamiliar way than where you were before."

That statement marked a pivotal moment in my understanding of the purpose of that season of illness when I felt like all hope was lost. It changed the view from negative to positive once more, reframed the trajectory of my decisions, and aided the management of my intentions about current experiences. The apostle then asked me to look at a biblical reference about the arrow and it would illuminate my understanding of what he said. I found one of those scriptures in the Old Testament.

> *And he has made My mouth like a sharp sword; In the shadow of His hand He has hidden Me, And made Me a polished shaft; In His quiver, He has hidden me (Isa. 49:2).*

Other translations refer to the arrow in this verse as the *polished arrow* or *choice shaft.* The prophet Isaiah metaphorically identified his role to deliver the weapon of the word of God to Judah and illustrated God's providence to protect and hide him "in the quiver." We can describe a quiver as a place of concealment until an appointed time. God's word is like an arrow that pierces the heart of everything it touches to create change. It goes directly to its target with intentional results (Heb. 4:12). Why an arrow? What is its significance to an understanding of seemingly negative life experiences?

An arrow was used in battles as an instrument of war. The Hebrew word for the arrow is *chets* and *chatsats.* An arrow symbolically refers to defense, protection, movement, force, swiftness, sureness, direction, and power. Wikipedia described the arrow as *"a fin-stabilized projectile that is launched from a bow and usually consists of a long, straight, stiff shaft with stabilizers called fletchings, as well as a weighty (and usually sharp and pointed) arrowhead attached to the front end, and a slot at the rear end called the nock for engaging the bowstring."*[13]

Each part of the arrow serves a specific function. For example, the *fin-fletching* (which is the end part of the arrow) provides lift, thrust, and the ability to steer and stabilize motion. The *arrowhead,* mostly made from stones or sharp objects, is used for piercing the target and is considered the deadliest part of the arrow. The bow is made with strings and used for launching the arrow. At the rear end of the arrow is a *nock* or slot, used for engaging the arrow with the bowstring in preparation for launching. The nock also controls the rotation of the arrow towards its target.

The arrow already possesses the ability to meet the intended target according to its design. However, the trajectory and strength of the arrow to meet the target depends on the steady, firm grip of the archer to place the *fletching* securely within the *nock*. Meeting the target also depends on extending the drawstring of the bow (backward) before the anticipated release to the intended target, to hit the bullseye.

Let me give some personal context to the above illustration. My medical diagnosis helped me redefine my life's purpose and set the stage for change. At the time of my challenge, I had to view the experience positively to glean God's purpose in my pain. Eventually, the setback gradually reaffirmed God's faithfulness to redirect my life towards His divine calling. Like an arrow, which inherently already embodied purpose, I was restrained so that the almighty archer could sharpen the arrowhead and complete any repairs to enhance the trajectory when it was time to be placed in the bow for another launch. My task was to submit to the all-knowing archer. Come on someone, just give me a loud **AMEN! HALLELUJAH!**

> *"An arrow can only be shot by pulling it backward. So, when life is dragging you back with difficulties, it means that it's going to launch you into something great."* (Unknown author).

In my research, I discovered that archery is a sophisticated sport that requires discipline, consistency, focus, technique, and precision. Anyone in the sport knows that choosing a bow depends on one's ability to manage the poundage and exhibit the strength for the drawback. Choosing the arrow depends on the draw length of the arrow and the archer's arm. In training, archers must have protective gear and the way they stand is critical for the ability to meet the target and remain safe. Some of the archer's first tasks are to have the perfect stance, know how to grip and draw the bow, be comfortable with the grip, accuracy, steady aim, and observe the wind or weather patterns. The tribe of Benjamin was known for producing efficient, expert, and skillful archers (1 Chron. 12:2). Those fighters, who were ambidextrous, were identified among the mighty warriors who fought with David against the armies of their enemies.

Each archer carries a quiver, which is a cylindrical container or a holding bag for the arrows. It is an important accessory. They prepare the arrows and hold them in the quiver and when it was time to launch the arrow, they pulled them out of the bag. Remember, a quiver is a place of concealment and safety for the arrow, waiting for the appointed time when the archer can use it. Remember Isaiah 49:2 "....*in his quiver hath he hid me.*" God is hiding you to renew, refresh and restore you for the launch. Do not be afraid, weary, or impatient with that process. David knew God's ability to protect and cover His people and the Psalms highlight many examples of his cry for help and dependence on God. He found a hiding place and solace in God.

> *For in the time of trouble He shall hide me in His pavilion;*
> *In the secret place of His tabernacle He shall hide me; He*
> *shall set me high upon a rock (Ps. 27:5).*

There was an ancient custom where offenders will go to the tabernacle or altar to hide. There they felt safe from their oppressors or pursuers. To date places of worship are considered places of safety or sanctuary cities for refugees and asylum seekers. Why the reference to the pavilion? The pavilion comes from the word **Papilio,**

connoting butterfly and means **to spread out like a cloth.**[14] It represented pillars with cloth stretched between them which gave shade
to guards who protected the palace, and anyone else seeking shelter.
In that location, no harm will come to them. God will shade, hide,
protect, and deliver His people from impending harm and danger,
and He will do the same for you. He will hide you in His quiver,
and you will be safe.

Colossians 3:3 tells us that **"For ye are dead, and your life is hid
with Christ in God."** The text speaks to our new place of security and
safety. With salvation and the new birth, Jesus Christ provides the
coverage we need to live a victorious Christian life. His shed blood
keeps us covered from, and through, sicknesses and diseases. The
new birth ensures our protection and deliverance in times of distress,
uncertainty, and danger. We do not need to be afraid of the storms
and trials that life brings to us. When we understand that no harm
can come to us unless God allows it, then we have a blessed assurance that we can conquer the enemies of our souls and be everything
God placed us on this earth to be. God is shaping the next course
of your journey and restoring greatness within your spirit, soul, and
body. He does it so that when you go out again, you would be effective
and accomplish His will with power and glory. Yield to the process
without holding back. Trust the Abba Father of your life.

Understanding the sport and battle strategy of the archer led to
an awareness of my journey and the object lesson it represented for
my future decisions and response to life's challenges and what may
look like a delay. The result was a shift in the representation of my
experiences, and I used the word recalibrate to describe my health
challenge. The word **recalibrate** did not originate with me but was
given to me by the Holy Spirit.

THE RECALIBRATING PROCESS

One day after I returned to Tobago from my first doctor's visit to the United States, I heard the Lord saying, ***"I am about to re-calibrate you"***. My husband works in mechanical engineering so while writing the book I asked him the meaning of the word. He explained that when something is loose, it must be tightened. Recalibrating is the adjusting process but you have to use an instrument for the task. **WOW!** That was so powerful! What a metaphor to amply describe my journey.

The Webster's Dictionary defines re-calibrate which is a derivative of the transitive verb calibrate.

To ***Re-calibrate*** is to calibrate something again.

To ***Calibrate*** is to:[15]

+ ascertain the caliber of something
+ determine, rectify, or mark the graduation of something (like temperature)
+ standardize something
+ adjust precisely for a particular function
+ measure precisely

Therefore, I understood that if God said He will recalibrate me it meant that He would check, adjust, create a new standard and rectify my spiritual temperature.

God who created me from my mother's womb, formed my inwards parts, carved me in the center of His palm (Ps. 139:14-17; Isa. 49:16; Jer. 1:5), knows my design. He wanted to fine-tune those areas that were out of alignment with His will for my life. The only way to achieve it was through those challenging circumstances that positioned me towards total dependence on Him. He desired to change some mindsets which limited me from functioning and walking in the capacity of my design. The recalibrating process was a redo, makeover, redesign, reshaping, and readjusting of what was lacking. When you are wholly committed to the Lord and doing His will God will sometimes take you through those seasons to redefine purpose.

> *Beloved, do not think it strange concerning the fiery trial which is to try you, as though some strange thing happened unto you (1 Pet. 4:12).*

I later added the words re-inventing to re-calibrate when people asked what was happening in my life. I would say the Lord is re-inventing me, or I am on a path of re-invention and re-calibration. When I spoke those words, many did not understand because some had already written me off as a failure. After all, I was not involved in full-time ministry anymore. They could not understand my journey. I should hasten to add that at first, it was difficult for me to embrace the terms and what they meant to my purpose-filled journey. I existed in the ethos of once you are on this vocation or career path you should stay with it until the end, to divert to something else suggested instability. I started feeling like a failure and measured my position by the standards and words of men. The darts were more forceful when they asked, "So you are not doing ministry again?" Or as one minister said, "She fire gone out!" and that hurt a lot and intensified the feelings of failure. Eventually, I realized you sometimes never end up where you intended to, and if you allow God to direct your steps and order your life it is an unpredictable journey. I accepted who I was and where I was in that season.

God called Abraham in his old age to leave a familiar land and journey to an unknown location (Gen. 12:1). In essence, Abraham had to re-invent himself at the age of seventy-five. Abram left Haran, the familiar and known place to journey with his wife Sarai (later called Sarah), nephew Lot, and some of his wealth and people to the land of Canaan. Note carefully that he did not make the journey alone, he carried people with him. We must be mindful that whenever God calls us to change it is always connected to people. Remember, when we resist the will of God when He calls us to change it affects the people around us also. We deprive them of the blessings available, which they can access by our obedience to God. It was after Abram left Haran; that he was renamed Abraham - the father of all nations for generations. He also received a son at the age of one hundred years, the promised seed to impact generations (Gen. 22:17). Age is important in many situations, but in God's economy of usefulness and purpose age cannot prevent Him from executing His will in our lives, when we yield to the leading of His Holy Spirit.

My warped thinking and mindset had to change and using the words re-calibrate and re-invent soothed the journey and made it less intense. I began to re-affirm that I was in the will of God, and He had the best for me because nothing that happens in my life surprises Him. Self-discovery started. My scars became my story, and I was not ashamed. Sometimes we try to hide the scars of our stories and negative experiences, but they matter because they define our struggles, tears, and triumphs. They tell our story. I have a scar on my forehead, you cannot miss it, and it tells a story. When I was a toddler my eldest brother and I were outdoor playing and he found a cutlass, took it, and pretended to be cutting grass. I walked up behind him and as he raised the machete, behind his head it struck me in the center of my forehead. The story could have been tragic, but whenever I look at it, the constant reminder is of God's protection.

CUTOFFS

There were some relationships I had to sever for this new journey. There were some counterfeit relationships that I thought would work on the new journey and God supernaturally cut them off. It was non-negotiable. I remember there was an occasion in the new journey people would call me to do ministry and I said no. Sometimes they begged and I still said no and offered referrals to other ministers. The season changed and I could not get carried away with the demands because God was doing something in me - creating newness, order, and healing. There was a time I recognized someone needed help and I saw it and told her. She asked can you help me. I said, "No I cannot help you at this time." It pained me to see others' facial reactions sometimes, but I could not give any more of myself. I knew that doing anything at that time would be a dishonor to God, myself, and the person because I could not give my best. God will require you to sever some connections which do not align with His will, during your re-calibrating process. Your response should be to yield to His will so that you can align with His will.

So, there I rested as an arrow within the strings of the bow, fully positioned within the 'nock' of the drawback, waiting for the relaunch. Meanwhile, the archer was sharpening the tips of my arrow. He stood poised, balancing my life, adjusting the aim, and making me comfortable within the drawback; just waiting, recalibrating, readjusting. Soon the relaunch would begin again, but for now, I waited, safe within the loving embrace and comforting, healing arms of my Saviour. I know you love the cushion of the familiar. Who does not? It is the safe zone. However, you must not allow the comfort zones to prevent you from the necessary changes which will lead to great rewards and access to what God has for you.

Discomfort is a good place to be if it will lead to creating a positive impact for life and eternity. Anyone who has experienced greatness always experiences the unfamiliar and uncomfortable. Embrace the discomfort that leads to renewal, healing, and restoration.

CHAPTER 8

The Love That Called Me

Home to Purpose

The Lord has appeared of old to me, saying: "Yes, I have loved you with an everlasting love; Therefore with lovingkindness, I have drawn you."

(Jer. 31:3)

Anyone who experienced *"being in love"* with another person is never the same. The feeling is indescribable and sometimes difficult to explain. Now, whether you misinterpreted love for lust and infatuation is a topic for another discussion. However, I am referring to genuine love, where there is respect, caring, compassion, empathy, forgiveness, and trust. The effect is greater after you first experience the counterfeit and then experience the genuine. The comparisons are unquestionably and undeniably vastly different. False love hurts, rejects, confuses, and destroys. True love brings peace, contentment, happiness, and freedom.

THE WOOING

In the scripture mentioned at the start of this chapter, Jeremiah referred to a love that is unchanging, everlasting, and sovereign. The expressions and outcome were dependent on the one offering and not merely on the actions of the one receiving. The prophet spoke of God's love for His chosen people Israel. A love which He demonstrated from the beginning, even when they did not deserve it because of their disobedience and rejection of His covenant authority and will. Earlier in the book of Jeremiah, God expressed His disappointment with the nation of Israel because they turned their hearts from Him. He said to them:

> *For My people have committed two evils: They have forsaken Me, the fountain of living waters, And hewn themselves cisterns--broken cisterns that can hold no water (Jer. 2:13).*

That love is eternal and without boundaries, surpassing thoughts, ideas, feelings, and nuances about qualification to receive it. The evidence of the boundless love expressed in the wooing, "*...with lovingkindness I have drawn thee*" is irrefutable. It is a love that calls one closer to, not away from. It speaks to drawing nearer, coming closer, and experiencing a new definition of intimacy, oneness, and purity. A love that calls one from the place of rejection and hopelessness. A love that lifts from the darkness into light, from the miry clay to the solid rock, from despair to hope, from limitations to limitless ability, from loss to gain, from fruitlessness to fruitfulness, from aimlessness to a purpose. Divine grace was extended to find its target and it will not release its' hold. It does not create room for negotiation of acceptance or rejection because of past events. It gently says, "here I am, come." Then it awaits a response.

The above describes the wooing of the Holy Spirit that is extended to the new believer, and the nature of the love that wooed me in the new season. When the Holy Spirit whispered that it was time to move, I gently acquiesced, even though I did not understand why, when, how, or what. When I said yes, there was a peace that all was well. I felt God's sovereign love for me as my *Abba* Father and knew that something better was in store for me. Was it difficult to uproot everything and say goodbye to a life I knew all my life? Of course, but I did not doubt that God was leading the way, and just as He promised to protect, guide, and direct my steps before, He certainly will now. Did I question God sometimes? Oh yes! I did! Sometimes there were responses and sometimes none, but I held fast to His word and directive. It was time to leave Tobago. In that season the love of God enfolded and surrounded me. He gave an assurance that *I was running towards my purpose not away from my pain and I was ready!* With faith restored, a soul at peace, and a heart set free, I reached for what lay ahead and set my sights on the path God already laid out for me. My hope fervently held to the truth that my heavenly father loved me before creation and therefore I can trust Him with me.

THE CHARACTER OF GOD'S LOVE

Love has a character of its own, and in some instances, the experiences of people shape their understanding and expression of love. They ultimately measure their experience of love from God according to those relationships. However, the love reflected by God to us has a distinct character that separates its expression from what is commonly identified in the world through social media influences and personal expressions. God said to the nation of Israel in the following scripture:

> *For the mountains shall depart and the hills be removed,*
> *But My kindness shall not depart from you, Nor shall My*
> *covenant of peace be removed." Says the Lord, who has*
> *mercy on you (Isa. 54:10).*

In Scripture, there are many Greek words denoting love. These include **agape** (God's unconditional love), **phileo** (love between friends), **eros** (romantic or sexual love), and **storge** (love between family members).[16] Though someone can exhibit more than one form of love in a relationship (such as a family having both storge and agape love), the highest form of love is agape and covers all the other expressions of love in any relationship, whether friendship, romantic or familial. **What then is the character of God's love for mankind?** I choose to describe God's love as incomprehensible, immeasurable, and purpose-filled.

A. **INCOMPREHENSIBLE**

To understand God's love with finite reasoning is an effort in futility since His love does not make a demand on the recipient. For this reason, the definition of God's love is **agape** (pure, wilful, and sacrificial love that intentionally seeks the highest good for another). This love transcends personality, status, and circumstances while embracing without discrimination and expectations. It looks beyond faults and sees needs. It can sometimes make us uncomfortable and inconvenience our priorities or expectations. That is the love God demonstrated and wants us to exhibit with others. Love is action-oriented and best understood when there is a demonstration accompanying the verbal expression. God demonstrated His love for mankind by sending Jesus Christ as the propitiation for sins.

> *For God so loved the world that He gave His only begotten*
> *Son, that whoever believes in Him should not perish but*
> *have everlasting life (John 3:16).*

> *Behold what manner of love the Father hath bestowed on*
> *us, that we should be called children of God (1 John 3:1).*

> *But God demonstrates His own love toward us, in that*
> *while we were still sinners, Christ died for us (Rom. 5:8).*

God loves us beyond human understanding and our finite minds cannot contain it.

> *For I am persuaded that neither death nor life, nor angels*
> *nor principalities nor powers, nor things present nor things*
> *to come, nor height nor depth, nor any other created thing,*
> *shall be able to separate us from the love of God which is*
> *in Christ Jesus our Lord (Rom. 8:38-39).*

There is nothing we can do or say to adequately describe God's love. His love reaches beyond everything negative, frustrating, and hopeless. His love will draw you out of that insecure place and love you into His purpose. Nothing can separate or hide you from His everlasting love.

B. **IMMEASURABLE**

Immeasurable speaks of the measureless, extensive, unfathomable, boundless, and interminable love of God that He extends to us. It goes on and on without end or boundaries. Just when you think you cannot get enough of God's love there is more available. God's love for you is unending and does not create boundaries because of your disposition or refusal to accept the love. It remains constant and cannot be measured or contained. It embodies and expresses His character, which is timeless and boundless.

> ...*God is love, and he who abides in love abides in God, and God in him (1 John 4:16).*

In an earlier chapter, I mentioned the prodigal son who came to himself after his choices produced consequences that demanded a change in perception (Luke 15:17). Prodigal means spending money or using resources in a wasteful manner. The Greek word for **prodigal** is **asotou** meaning **extravagant** or **wasteful**. Here was a son who did not consider the cost of his father's wealth but wasted it at the first opportunity and later returned broken and empty. However, what was more significant about the discourse in the parable is the father's visible and tangible response of acceptance and forgiveness. Love required empathy (what we call unconditional positive regard in counseling and therapy) far beyond the reaches of human comprehension. Love requires a steadfastness that is not dependent on the reciprocity of the recipient, though one hopes that they would show love and respect in return. It is without exception or discrimination. It says come and come boldly to receive love's call.

Through the Lord's mercies, we are not consumed, Because
His compassions fail not. They are new every morning;
Great is Your faithfulness (Lam. 3:22-23).

One of the assurances we have about God's love is that it will be with us forever and nothing can separate us from His love (Rom. 8:38-39). Whatever we do in disobedience does not diminish His love for us also.

Yet in all these things we are more than conquerors through
Him who loved us (Rom. 8:37).

His sacrifice on the cross covers our sins and shortcomings and reminds us that we always have access to receive restoration and healing. He constantly reminds us that in everything we can surmount the challenges because of His love for us.

C. **PURPOSEFILLED**

There is an aspect of God's love that directs us to His will which can sometimes seem harmful, and we may become resistant. However, the objective is to lead us to fulfill His divine purpose. I could not complete this chapter without creating a balance so that you will not close this book with the illusion that the God who loves us would not correct our disobedience and rebellion. To do that would deny the truth of Scripture and create a deception about the nature of the love which desires to call you home as it called me home. *So yes, the character of God's love is purposeful, even in the chastening, you may be experiencing right now!*

For whom the Lord loves He chastens, And scourges every son whom He receives (Heb. 12:6).

As many as I love, I rebuke and chasten. Therefore be zealous and repent (Rev. 3:19).

When God desires to restore wholeness in us, the methods can sometimes seem harsh, but the intention is restoration and reconciliation. In the scripture mentioned above the writer of the epistle, who is Paul, introduced the concept of chastening by referring to a relationship between a father and son to signify what happens when there is discipline. The intention of discipline is not only punitive, but to encourage and restore right behavior, and when applied correctly it enhances the relationship and maintains mutual respect. God will chasten us through the different circumstances and events He allows when we walk in disobedience. Sometimes we may reap the consequences of those choices because of the laws of nature associated with retribution. After the chastening, His love will embrace, heal, and restore you.

RETURN TO YOUR FIRST LOVE

When we replace our love for God with people, things, and events, it robs us of the blessing of communion (*fellowship - koinonia*) with Him. He allows the consequences of our waywardness to redirect us back to His loving embrace. God redirected me to Him - my first love. I got busy with work, ministry, and family issues and neglected to stay connected to the source of love that fuelled my passion and purpose. God's love pulled me back in my season of waiting. His love called me home to His presence - home to my first love. That is what He said through the Apostle John to the New Testament Church represented in the eschatological biblical book of Revelation. The church represented there was a Church that lost focus and purpose for being and doing. They had the works but lacked a relationship with God. God's formula for a redefinition of their purpose was a return to loving God and those things which symbolized His will. Again, not doing (works) but being (building relationship).

> *Nevertheless I have this against you, that you have left your first love (Rev. 2:4).*

God always demonstrates His love through action and used the Old Testament book of Hosea to demonstrate His love for the nation of Israel. Throughout the book of Hosea, God demonstrated that He always goes after the ones He loves - His people called by His name. God's intent is always the restoration of the covenant relationship because He is a covenant-keeping God. According to His nature, He keeps His word and promised never to leave or forsake us (Heb. 13:5). He will do that even if it means that He will seek us out, find us, and restore us when we break our promises and turn away in rebellion and disobedience. He stands by His word and will do what He said.

> *The grass withers, the flowers fades, but the word of our God stands forever (Isa. 40:8).*

> *So shall My word be that goes forth from My mouth; It shall not return to Me void, But it shall accomplish what I please, And I shall prosper in the thing for which I sent it (Isa. 55:11).*

Hosea was a prophet and God told him to marry a prostitute who left him and was unfaithful to him repeatedly. However, every time she left her matrimonial home God told Hosea to go after her. This demonstrates unwavering, steadfast, relentless love, which will not stop until the receiver of that love is fully restored in its embrace. That place of safety, security, wholeness, freedom, and purpose.

That was the love that the father of the prodigal son had for him and demonstrated when he returned home (Luke 15:11-32). He welcomed his son into his loving embrace, and it did not matter that he disrespected, abandoned, and embarrassed his family. What mattered most to his father was that he was home. It was difficult for his older brother to understand the extravagance of the celebration because of the character of love displayed by his father. Such is the love God exhibits to His children when we turn our hearts towards the lover of our souls. We experience spiritual intimacy once again and are swept away by a love that does not remember the wrong done, but compassionately considers the possibility of a future (Micah 7:19). That gesture of forgetting our sins exhibits the unfathomable grace of a gracious father.

Intimacy is described as the process of knowing oneself in the presence of another. When we fall into the arms of a loving God, we experience true intimacy and in the place of safety and trust, we experience peace and do not desire to wander anymore. He reassures us of our limitless possibilities, regardless of our past. We feel confident to take on the world and all its battles because of **HE** who stands with us - **A loving father.** That is the power of *Agape* love that will enfold you when love calls you home and you return to its embrace.

LOVE OF ANOTHER KIND

I recall the farewell service held by my local church in Tobago on the final Sunday of August 2015, when some believers made pronouncements about marriage. The summary of what they said referred to their belief that when I migrate the Lord will bless me with a husband. My response? Laughter. Yes, laughter. I laughed just as Sarah laughed when God said she would have a baby at age seventy-five (Gen. 18:12). Why? Well because I grew accustomed to having failed relationships and was exhausted with the cycle. I concluded that for the next years of my life I would focus on myself and doing what God wanted. When I traveled to the United States the thoughts of marriage were insignificant to my goals, but not God's. In my case, God required obedience to reposition from the familiar and launch out into the unfamiliar. I entered the United States in September 2015 and God had a surprise waiting for me that blew my mind. What is impossible with man is possible with God (Matt. 19:26; Mark 10:27).

There was a message on my Messenger account from someone unfamiliar asking if I was the same Anne-Marie from Secondary School, I asked who was asking and once the person mentioned their name I responded, "Yes." That person is my husband today. He found me and pulled me into love's embrace.

> Let him lead me to the banquet hall, and let his banner
> over me be love (Song of Solomon 2:4).

We were married within three months (something I will not recommend for the emotionally weak, immature, and faint-hearted). My husband and I knew each other from secondary school when we were adolescents. He liked me at that time, but my focus was not on a relationship, we were children. To me, it was just normal teenage infatuation. After Secondary school, we went our separate ways, and I did not see or hear from or about him for over thirty years. I later found out that sometimes when he traveled to Tobago, he would enquire about me or search for me, but some mutual friends never gave him an affirmative response. Of course, I was busy with ministry and service to God and did not remember him since we did not have a relationship before. Before and after marriage many of my family members and friends were in shock and disbelief about how events unfolded. They asked, "How and when did this happen?" I do not think they were in more disbelief than I was. Some suggested that my husband existed as a secret part of my life before I migrated and that was why I left for the United States. When God does a miracle, it always leaves waves of cynicism, skepticism, and consternation.

LOVES' WAY

Isn't it amazing that when God has something for you, He shifts everything so that you will receive that blessing? And isn't it amazing that it does not matter where you are or your age and status in life? **GOD'S LOVE WILL FIND YOU AND TRUE LOVE WILL FIND YOU!** Love found me! I cannot say that I found love because I was not looking for love at the time. That love called me into a place of physical rest and wholeness when I embraced it. I fell into love's embrace and knew that it was the beginning of another season of my life. God moved me from Tobago to the United States to meet the love of my life and the one who would be my support - for the next journey of life, for the rest of my life. I wondered what would have been my story if I did not walk into obedience. What if I did not say yes to the voice of the Holy Spirit when he said it was time to leave my comfort zone and journey into an unknown place? God rewards obedience, faithfulness, and confidence in His word.

I thought my move was just about health and vocation and making a way for others, I did not know it would also be about love. We can never predict the blessings of obedience, but we know that when we obey, God responds. He holds them in His archives of your life and at the right time, He releases the rewards. Sometimes when God chooses to manifest His will and presence it may not look like what we anticipated. What I know is that when we are separated to fulfil a purpose, we will not understand His ways, but we can trust Him because He is **'Jehovah El Roi'** the God who sees us.

CHAPTER 9

Repositioning to Excellence in the Journey

But we have this treasure in jars of clay to show that this all-surpassing power is from God and not from us.

(2 Cor. 4:7)

God endowed believers (who are His servants and ministers) with a unique opportunity to carry His anointing to impact individuals and generations. God does that despite our natural and carnal limitations and stipulates how we must accomplish His will. His formula was not self-reliance but God-dependent. When we recognize that our potential for expansion is limitless then we become dependent on God's ability and the enabling power of the Holy Spirit in us. After that realization, we become unstoppable. The minute we shift our gaze from God or decide to do God's will with our finite understanding we would eventually crash, even though we may have a good start. All that we are and hope to be resides in Him. Paul, the writer of the text above knew that and he penned the words:

For in him we live and move and have our being...
(Acts 17:28).

The Biblical commentator Matthew Henry said, "*In him, we live; that is, the continuance of our lives is owing to him and the constant influence of his providence…it is by the uninterrupted concourse of his providence that our souls move in their outgoings and operations, that our thoughts run to and fro about a thousand subjects, and our affections run out towards their proper objects.*" [17]

In Christ we exist, without him, we do not exist! Just imagine that without him our existence is fiction, useless, meaningless, and unrealistic. We must remain intimately connected to our life source, the one who created and made us after His image and likeness and breathed the **pneuma** (word of life – His life-giving force) into us (Gen. 1:27; 2: 7).

The Apostle Paul further stated:

I have been crucified with Christ and I no longer live, but Christ lives in me. The life I now live in the body, I live by faith in the Son of God, who loved me and gave Himself for me (Gal. 2:20).

God called us as His earthly treasure to demonstrate His glory throughout the earth. We are the treasure that He encased with clay. We are His treasure which He created in His image and likeness. Sin created separation and distortion, but through the shed blood of Jesus Christ on the cross, He secured salvation and restoration of the glory which He intended from the beginning of creation. People do not see an earthly physical manifestation of God on the earth, but they see Him through us when we exhibit His character. As we conduct our daily activities, accomplish tasks, and navigate relationships with other people, we should express the image of God and the nature of Christ living within us. He called us royal, chosen, and peculiar.

> *But you are a chosen people, a royal priesthood, a holy nation, God's special possession, that you may declare the praises of him who called you out of darkness into his wonderful light (1 Peter 2:9).*

After restoration and healing, something changes. Nothing remains the same, and it is important to do everything possible to maintain that change. Doing that helps to prevent a regression to the former habits or situations which incubated the patterns of dysfunction or contributed to the former crisis. A lesson learned sets the pace for future decisions. Therefore, in the new season of healing and restoration, I focused my heart on gleaning from God's treasure chest of wisdom and knowledge, for my journey of newness.

One of the first tasks when I embraced *"the love which called me home,"* was to reconsider my circle of influence. Yes, you heard me correctly. I asked the questions: "Who are the people around me that exhibit the major influences in my life? How do they contribute or not to my restoration and healing? How do I see them influencing my life in the future? Are those people God ordained or stumbling blocks?" My determination was, to re-establish Godly connections because I knew I had some ungodly connections which stood in my way of accomplishing God's purpose. Whether they agreed or not it was a done deal. Whether I felt good, hesitant, or uncomfortable about it, was not an option. My survival depended on that decision, and I knew I was not in control and could not dictate the course of my destiny. Only God can. I needed Godly counsel around me, those who would be destiny helpers and not destiny blockers. Those who would say, "Thus saith the Lord" and it is so. Those who would be willing to walk the journey with me despite the sacrifice. Godly counsel and destiny helpers are critical components for our spiritual growth and advancement.

> *For lack of guidance a nation falls, but victory is won through many advisers (Prov. 11:14).*

Without Godly influences, we may fight some battles that we do not need to fight. Others went before us, fought for us, and can help to cushion and direct the course of our journey, under the mighty hand of God. Remember Joseph's words:

> *But God sent me ahead of you to preserve for you a remnant on earth and to save your lives by a great deliverance (Gen. 45:7).*

Those who went before you and know the way, will guide you and stand with you. I had many mentors in my earthly and spiritual journey and many currently influence my destiny. Some may not be active in my life presently, but I carry their influence with me on this journey. Mentoring is an essential spiritual principle and a necessary component of your journey if you want to be successful. The role sometimes changes where you can become the mentor after being or while being mentored by others. I encourage you to submit to mentoring so that you can grow and blossom in your earthly and spiritual journey.

THE IMPORTANCE OF FOSTERING HEALTHY CONNECTIONS

John Maxwell has a book entitled *"Everyone Communicates: Few Connect."*[18] Connection influences your ability to fulfill your purpose. Fulfilling your purpose is attached to people and relationships. We must understand that everyone who crosses our path has something to offer. Though no one is perfect, there is good and bad in all of us, but our expectations in that relationship influence the outcome. Some people may be temporary fixtures in our lives while others may be permanent, but we must know the difference.

The word connection comes from the word **connect** which is to **link or join.** The word connection means *"A relationship in which a person, thing, or idea is linked or associated with something else".*[19] It speaks to affinity, association, kinship, liaison, and linkage. Picture a chain, some links connect the chain to make it a whole instrument for use. If one link is out of place or misshaped it affects the chain's ability to remain connected. If you are in the wrong connection it would show up somewhere, somehow in your accomplishments. The Greek word for connection is **syndesi** which means attachment, another meaning is **koinotita** meaning communication, that same root word gives us **koinonia - fellowship.**[20] When translated in English **syndikos** means **syndication - which speaks to the concept of an association.**[21] There must be a commonality of vision between you and your human connections. You need an association of people around you with the same mindset that God has towards you, to accomplish His will. Those people must also be in communion with God to hear from Him concerning their life.

How do you recognize unhealthy connections? Observe instances of abuse, control, humiliation, lack of quality time or availability, the pressure to do something you do not want to do, and unpredictable behavior with negative outcomes. Contrast those behaviors with healthy connections which exemplify trust, support, safety, respect, honesty, equality, the ability to be yourself, and good communication. The right connection matters in your journey of healing and restoration.

Do two walk together unless they have agreed to do so? (Amos 3:3).

Sometimes the connections we despise and run away from may just be the ones to get us to where we should be, and those that we crave elude us because it is not in God's sovereign will for us. When you are struggling to understand your reason for being it is difficult to create healthy connections and get the best from those existing relationships. The connections we seek are multidimensional and include connections with God, family members, spouses, friends, work colleagues, and business partners. Those connections create a community of support and caring to succor us through difficulties and cultivate an atmosphere of happiness, wholeness, and catharsis.

GODLY CONNECTIONS

When Abraham started on his journey to another land as God called him to do, he encountered many stumbling blocks, and some of those blockages were directly related to his connections. One of the connections was with his nephew Lot who was not the vision bearer of the promise. We must be careful to remember that the calling and the vocation were given to us by God and not the people around us. Other people will have an opinion and ideas about what we should do and how it must be done. It is God's word that stands secure and would affirm us in the moments when we feel abandoned, empty, alone, and our faith begins to waver. Ensure that you have someone who can stand with you in the times when your faith is tested, and you feel insecure about God's calling and promises for you. If you do not, it can be the difference between life and death.

Let us get back to Lot. Lot traveled with Abraham on the journey until the time when Lot was in opposition to Abraham's purpose and hope for a better tomorrow, then Abraham chose to leave him behind (Gen. 13:1-18). Though Lot was family (Abraham's nephew), Abraham made a choice that Lot will not hinder God's promise to him and his generations. Similarly, some connections open doors of blessings, grace, and favor.

Sarai, Abram's wife was a blessing when Abraham decided that she would be a buffer between him and Pharaoh as they passed through Egypt, though Abraham lied that she was his sister. Pharaoh did not deal harshly with them because of Sarai and the diseases the Lord inflicted against his house when they kept her (Gen. 12: 10-20). Lot's wife brought destruction to his house because she did not want to release the ungodly lifestyle of Sodom and Gomorrah, where they settled after the dispute with Abraham. Even at a time of impending destruction when God destroyed the land of Sodom and Gomorrah by fire, she preferred and desired the benefits of the ungodly land, turned into a pillar of salt, and died there (Gen. 19:26). Lot's choices also produced generational curses and resulted in the birth of the land of Moab and Ammon (which today is in Jordan). The Moabites and Ammonites were enemies of Israel and Judah and constantly besieged and prevented them from occupying territories. There was a generational impact. It is not only about the friends you choose but it is also extended to your choice of a marriage partner or a business associate. Certainly, you cannot choose your family members, but sometimes you must choose how close you hold them to your dreams if their influence would perpetuate a negative dysfunctional pattern and sabotage your destiny in Christ.

The Lord commands His blessings when there is a union of purpose and pursuit, and a community of shared beliefs, vision, and dreams, though it may manifest in various ways. It does not denote the absence of disagreements but signifies oneness which creates the catalyst for generational blessings.

> *How good and pleasant it is when God's people live together in unity! It is like precious oil poured on the head, running down on the beard, running down on Aaron's beard, down on the collar of his robe. It is as if the dew of Hermon, were falling on Mount Zion. For there the Lord bestows His blessing, even life for evermore (Psalm 133:1-3).*

Have you noticed that within Scripture, when God called an individual to greatness, he always connected them to someone else before they launched out? That person can usher them into or carry them through that season. Again, if you examined the Scriptures, you would observe that for any significant event or monumental task, there was a connection to people and nations. Of course, it can be both positive and negative influences. Let me show you what I mean. Joshua had a Moses, Elisha had an Elijah, Jonathan had a David, the disciples had Jesus, Mary (the mother of Jesus) had an Elizabeth, and Timothy had his mother and grandmother. That is God's divine order at work. The Towel of Babel progressed and survived before God destroyed it because of the cohesiveness in the vision and mindset of the people (Gen. 11:1-9). The Bible records that they said, **"…let us build…, let us make …"** (Gen. 11:4), and God saw it. From the start of creation, God said, **"…LET US…"** (Gen. 1:26). Power of agreement in the Godhead initiated activities and events that set the course for the future hope for humanity. Similarly, the wrong association between humanity and the enemy led to the spiritual death of humanity (Gen. 3:1). Power of agreement went to work again with the act of redemption for mankind and now we have eternal hope. God established that order for the Church to maintain and fulfill His will and He established connections through the leadership and spiritual gifts to the body.

> *So Christ himself gave the apostles, the prophets, the evangelists, the pastors, and teachers, to equip his people for works of service, so that the body of Christ may be built up until we all reach unity in the faith, and in the knowledge of the Son of God and become mature, attaining to the whole measure of the fullness of Christ (Eph. 4:11-13).*

Godly connections foster hope and produce generational impact. It is not only about who is our friend, but who exhibits the potential for Godly influence and generational blessings. Enquiring from God about who should be the people in our inner circle with the authority to speak into our lives, and share the vision and purpose of our lives, must be a priority. Those connections become catalysts or bridges to fulfilled purposes. Creating healthy connections requires wholeness and a general understanding that there is an existing reciprocal relationship and expectations within that connection.

FOR THE PEOPLE

There is a phrase within the preamble of the United States Constitution that denotes the heart of governmental service and governance. The phrase is *"We the People"* and demonstrates that the ultimate source of constitutional power is not the elected governing body but the people. The embodiment of the Constitution presupposes those decisions which the constitution allows to give the political will to the government on behalf of its citizens for its citizens or "the people." The words endorse the belief that the government will work for the people and that the people will have a significant contribution to the process of governance. The reason why this analogy is significant in this chapter on connections is when we recognize that we cannot exist without connections, we also understand that our connections provide the impetus for the accomplishment of our vocation. This happens on behalf of others and for others. We also recognize that we do not accomplish healing and restoration for ourselves but also for the healing and restoration of others. Jesus Christ said something significant to Simon Peter before he made a profound statement about the rock and the church.

> *Simon, Simon, Satan has asked to sift all of you as wheat. But I have prayed for you, Simon, that your faith may not fail. And when you have turned back, strengthen your brother (Luke 22:31-32).*

Jesus Christ wanted Simon Peter to know that his healing and restoration were a key resource to the healing and restoration of others. Our healing and restoration also connect us to those in need of the same.

My healing and restoration represent powerful tools for ministry and in my work with individuals, families, and couples as a marriage and family therapist. It reassures me of the unlimited capacity of an individual to develop strategies and make choices to change circumstances and surmount challenges they will encounter.

CHAPTER 10

A New Season at Home

> There is a time for everything, and a season for every
> activity under the heaven.... He has made everything
> beautiful in its time. He has also set eternity in the human
> heart; yet no one can fathom what God has done from
> beginning to end.

(Ecclesiastes 3:1-11)

As I am writing this book I feel as though I am living my second life, or it can probably be my third since I almost died before birth if the devil had his way. *I live under an open heaven of grace, favor, blessings, overflow, and breakthrough (promises the Lord gave me in January 2021).* I am grateful to God for the life He gave me now and believe that He made an investment in me and I do not want to let Him down. I often say reflectively that God is looking for His returns, but His response to me does not depend on my willingness to reciprocate His grace and favor. How can we live in this new season when we return home to the lover of our souls? There are some pre-requisites to living fully in the embrace of the new season of love and enjoying the moments with the person we love. Our response in our relationship with God - the lover of our souls should be the same. It is similar to how a person in love functions with their mate in the initial throes of love. There is limitless trust, expressions of endearment, and gratitude, and you find rest in that place of safety. God wants His children to find that place of intimacy, where we know Him and know who we are so that we do not have to leave home anymore. Where we know that we are covered and do not have to be afraid and find peace in who we are and where He is taking us.

TRUSTING COMPLETELY

To trust is to have an unconditional, confident dependence, hope, and belief in someone or something without restraint or reservation.[22] I know He is my *Jehovah El Roi*. The term *El Roi* is one of the names of God and in Hebrew translates as *"shepherd or as seeing, looking or gazing."*[23] God looks out for you, even when others do not look out for you. He sees you and covers you when others do not. His gaze is fixed on you when others overlook you and you feel pushed aside and forgotten. It is like a child who is outdoors at the park with their parents and decides to go off and play. The parent's primary focus is on their children, to ensure they are protected and do not go off wandering on their own to be exposed to any dangerous situations.

The mention of *Jehovah El Roi* occurs only once in the Scripture and introduced another attribute of God in the Genesis narrative of Abraham, Sarah, and the Egyptian maid Hagar. Hagar had a child with Abraham through the insistence of Sarah and her lack of faith that God will give them a promised seed as He said. While Hagar was pregnant with the child (Ishmael) Sarah dealt harshly with her and she fled from the house. While alone in the wilderness, resting at a well, the angel of the Lord spoke with her and sent her back to Abraham's house. She marveled that God saw her, an Egyptian, a bondservant, and spoke with her, so she named the well *Beer-lahai-roi - He sees me*, as her thanksgiving to God (Gen. 16:14).

It is also interesting that Hagar said, *"I have now seen the one who sees me"* (Gen. 16:14) after her encounter with the angel. There is a level of intimacy that we experience when we look into the face of the one who confronts us about ourselves and who sees our *nakedness*. Nakedness here means full disclosure and an unhinged pre-disposition. Normally when that happens you have two options, stay open and transparent, or run away and hide. However, there is value in understanding intimacy between two people who love each other. True intimacy allows you to be in the presence of another person and know yourself through their eyes. That knowing is responsible for *casting off all restraint* or *exhibiting transparency*. You will notice in the Old Testament that there is an absence of any description of a formal marriage ceremony according to what we know in present-day culture. What you will see are terms like *"he went in unto her"* and *"knew her"* (Gen. 4:1; Matt. 1:25). The word *"knew"* refers to the consummation of the marriage, and it speaks of intimacy. To be intimate speaks to connection and oneness.

When there is an intimacy between you and the one who calls you home, there will be complete trust. There is an openness to allow the mirror of love to reflect the true feelings that want to hide on the inside.

> *You will keep in perfect peace those whose minds are steadfast, because they trust in You (Isa. 26:3).*

You can trust completely in the one who sees you and will never leave or forsake you (Heb. 13:5). His name is Immanuel "God with us" (Isa. 7:4; Matt. 1:23). The one who records our tears and bottles them (Psa. 58: 8). The one who said we are the apple of His eyes (Psa.

17:8). The one who said you do not have to be afraid because He will go before you to make your way prosperous (Deut. 31:6-8; Isa. 41:10-13). Faith in God requires **knowing,** and that knowing occurs when there is uncertainty in your life and you have to trust God completely because there is nothing else that you can do. The knowledge that He is who He says He is and will do what He says He will, is what will sustain you at that moment. When you come to yourself, know who you are, whose you are, who you serve, and His ability through you, then you can become an unstoppable force. You do not fear, and there is nothing that can hold you back. You speak and walk with confidence and boldness and know that you can do anything. Then you can say with a full understanding:

> *With your help I can advance against a troop; with my*
> *God I can scale a wall (Ps. 18:29).*

The lovingkindness of God would not permit you to go unnoticed, even if it means that He will change the course of events and rigidity of customs and order to get you into a place of assurance and peace. Therefore, you can trust that He would not leave you hopeless. His Word is truth, which is the essence of His divine nature, so you can trust in Him.

> *…I am the way, the truth and life…(John 14:6).*

We trust Him because in Him is everything we need that is sufficient for our life on earth, and to prepare us for life eternally.

> *His divine power has given us everything we need for a*
> *godly life through our knowledge of him who called us by*
> *his own glory and goodness (2 Peter 1:3).*

There is a pre-requisite to accessing His blessings on your life. God distributes to us **all things** as we trust and depend upon Him. It is through Christ and in Christ that there is a response for the believer. The Pauline Epistles carry a theme that the Biblical scholars identify as the **EN CHRISTO** theme. *'En Christo'* is the Greek derivative for *In Christ.* There are several references to the believer's status in Christ and the need for trusting in Christ for the demonstration of the work of salvation, reconciliation, and consecration. We must trust Him wholeheartedly because in Him we are forgiven, accepted, and loved.

> *Trust in the Lord with all your heart and lean not on your own understanding; in all your ways submit to him, and he will make your paths straight (Prov. 3:5-6).*

You must remain hopeful that God has your back and I know He is waiting on you to trust Him completely.

DEMONSTRATING FORGIVENESS

Forgiveness is an act of the will in response to true repentance and obedience. An act that says I understand the many times I received grace and forgiveness from others. An act that says I understand the importance of forgiveness in healing and restoration. To forgive is to forgive not only others but myself because I know that I am deserving of forgiveness, and I want to experience a rebirth. Rebirth becomes possible with an acknowledgment of how my experiences and choices affect my current functioning. If you must embrace the benefits of healing and restoration you must be willing to forgive. Forgiveness is never easy. It pains and hurts but the release is always indescribable. Therapeutically, forgiveness is a critical component in the process of catharsis with all who experienced trauma and pain. Throughout my experience as a minister and therapist, I counseled couples who experienced infidelity and violation of trust and saw the difficulty with forgiveness. The pain was intense, but for those who eventually got to that place, the restoration was exciting and pure.

Jesus Christ, in the Lord's prayer, implored that we should forgive others, as he forgave us (Matt. 6:12-15). Forgiving others is a precondition for our forgiveness. We do that from a position of knowing that we need grace and forgiveness because no one is perfect. All of us sinned and made a mockery of God's glory embodied in our creative being (Rom. 3:23). When we do not forgive it becomes a hindrance to prayer and access to God's divine promises, which is one of the reasons why forgiveness is not only for others but for us. Some people will say, "I cannot forgive that person who hurt me," but God is the one who gives us the capacity to forgive.

> *Be kind and compassionate to one another, forgiving each*
> *other, just as in Christ God forgave you (Eph. 4:32).*

Before you start your new journey please forgive. As you continue your journey, forgive. It is difficult to forget, and it may be necessary to remember to avoid some unhealthy situations. However, you can forgive and trust God to give you the grace to love others from a place of purity and empathy. God is asking you today to forgive so that you can start or continue your journey. **YOU CAN DO IT!**

PRACTICING GRATITUDE

Practicing gratitude is another way of embracing this new season at home, in your heart, and with your Saviour. Gratitude to God and others is not a selective process of human existence, it is a prerequisite for a fulfilled life. Gratitude changes our posture and prepares us for continuity. When we acknowledge that we are not the conductor of the music in our lives, we would exhibit gratitude with the understanding that we are not here by chance but by divine purpose. We will also understand that we are instruments in God's hands. I like to say that gratitude keeps me humble and grounded.

> *Give thanks in all circumstances: for this is God's will for you in Christ Jesus (1 Thess. 5:18)*

When the storms of life and the strong winds of despair and discouragement starts surrounding you, remember to be grateful. That may mean finding a song of gratitude through Psalms, hymns, and spiritual songs. Sing a song of thanksgiving, sing a song of gratitude (Ps. 96:1). A song will lift you out of fear and depression when you do not know how to pray. Worship will take you into the presence of God and silence every doubt that encloses you in its grasp.

> *Sing to the LORD a new song, for he has done marvelous things; his right hand and his holy arm have worked salvation for him (Ps. 98:1).*

Isn't it common that one can so easily forget the events which precipitated one's success or new prestigious position in life? There is a colloquial saying that I often heard my parents and other elderly people in my family using: *"Never damn the bridge that you crossed."* Another one is *"Don't forget where you came from."* Both sayings implore the practicing of gratitude as a way of life because you endorse where you came from and the people who were responsible for contributing to where you are currently. Ingratitude destroys relationships and exposes the heart of the perpetrator. It is a characteristic that pushes people from your life and hinders you from accessing the blessings and favors those relationships can provide.

Jesus Christ in his teachings also highlighted the importance of practicing gratitude by using an object lesson after he healed ten lepers and only one returned to say thank you (Luke 17:11-19). Implicit in the story is the pervasiveness of ingratitude when one examines the ratio of those who received healing, in comparison to only one who returned to say thank you. Human nature is generally ungrateful unless there are belief and value systems to hold us accountable for the necessity of gratitude. One can speculate about the motive of the nine ungrateful lepers, but to practice gratitude, requires an ability to get outside of oneself. Ok, let me simplify it for you. I mean to forget about yourself, your needs, who you are, and what you want - humility. Yes, humility lifts you from self-preservation and self-interest to esteeming another, reaching out to another, or accepting help from another, realizing that you do not possess all the answers and *"No man is an island."*

In my experience, expressing gratitude to God changes my reaction to adverse circumstances. It is cathartic and introduces peace and grace, while putting into perspective what matters and what does not, at that time. It opens the door to allow the light into your life and dispels the darkness of frustration and insufficiency. I tend to feel less burdened by what is happening around me when I express gratitude. My outlook on the experience changes immediately when I shift from what I do not have and begin contemplating what I have or past events when I experienced the goodness of God. There is a sudden metamorphosis. The boundaries shift from the immediacy of the need and extend beyond the visible to the potential for the supernatural manifestation of God in tangible ways. When you practice gratitude, it drives a nail in the coffin of fear and doubt, seals their fate in your life once and for all, and you receive wholeness.

RESTING IN HIS REST

There is an old saying **"Home is where the heart is."** Though no one knows the origin of the saying, there is a version that identifies the words as **"Home is where the hearth is."** The word hearth refers to a fireplace, which provides warmth and safety from the cold.[24] Therefore, they attribute the metaphorical use of hearth in the saying to mean - one's heart finds a home in a place that may not be where you were born or a mere building, but any place where there is warmth, caring, acceptance and safety. So, wherever your heart finds warmth, peace and safety is home. We know that is true because some people do not find those characteristics in their home, but they find them among other people and substitute places.

I may not know the origins of the proverb, but I know it is true and relevant to the experiences of many. Home and love are inextricably connected because where you feel at home is dependent on whether you feel loved. When you feel loved you feel safe. The heart is the center of one's being, the soul, the place of peace and solitude. The place where you rest before it can manifest in the physical. The word rest defined is as *"cease work or movement, relax, refresh oneself, or recover strength"*.[25] Rest is an important prerequisite for healthy physical functioning and stability of the heart, and mind. It is an essential daily component of a person who is at peace with themselves and understands the value of self-care. When there is restoration and healing, it is important to factor rest into one's daily schedule, maintain the gains of previous healing, and capitalize on the benefits of future endeavors. Since a new season demands a changed response, then rest must be an important equation in the functioning of a restored heart.

Rest was always at the center of God's heart for His chosen people from the start of creation. God rested on the seventh day. God rested not because He was tired but because His creative work was finished.

> *By the seventh day God had finished the work he had been doing; so on the seventh day he rested from all his work. Then God blessed the seventh day and made it holy, because on it he rested from all the work of creating that he had done (Gen. 2:2-3).*

If God rested, why do we think we are exempted from rest? Jesus also rested during his earthly ministry (Mark 4:38).

> *Then, because so many people were coming and going that they did not even have a chance to eat, he said to them, "Come with me by yourselves to a quiet place and get some rest." (Mark 6:31).*

Jesus rested because he was tired since he had a human nature. Though he had a divine nature he was also subject to human emotions including tiredness. We must understand the distinction. Jesus therefore, modeled both spiritual and physical resting. Spiritually, to revive his soul and receive instruction and sustenance from God, and because his Father's sovereign will was his ultimate desire. Physically to replenish his physical body. God's desire for the children of Israel as He led them through the wilderness was to find a place of rest. However, they did not understand that the rest was not only a physical place but also a symbolic representation of the eternal rest God provides for His children who trust Him.

So I declared an oath in my anger, 'They shall never enter my rest.'… So we see that they were not able to enter, because of their unbelief (Heb. 3:11-19).

Through Jesus' sacrifice on the cross, we can receive His rest in this dispensation of grace. Spiritual rest is a secret place in God where our soul is renewed daily, and our faith is re-affirmed about His intention in our lives. A place where the Holy Spirit has full access to restore and renew our tired souls, and we yield to his wooing. We must rest because of our human limitations, and we entered the rest of God through faith. We must rest knowing that God has the final say and we can do nothing to accomplish His will on the earth in our physical ability but need the **dunamis** power and supernatural ability of God to fulfill His purpose.

In the universally accepted and notable **Shepherd's Psalm** the writer David, who was also a shepherd said:

He makes me lie down in green pasture: he leads me beside quiet water, he refreshes my soul. He guides me along the right paths for his name's sake (Ps. 23:2-3).

David was a shepherd who understood the value of rest for the weary shepherd. One of the central responsibilities of a shepherd is the welfare of his flock. Other responsibilities include protecting them from predators, monitoring their health, and shearing the flock. The shepherd must be on call just in case there is an urgent matter concerning the flock. Most shepherds lived close to the flock and would take them out to grazing areas early in the morning and then return them to their primary pasture at night. Though most shepherds had guard dogs, the shepherd kept a watchful eye for everything that could compromise the flock, including injuries with the potential to cause diseases. He watched over the sheep who were pregnant with ewes and ready for the delivery of young ones. There were constant welfare checks on the lambs. All those daily responsibilities would be tiring for a shepherd.

A shepherd would need rest to function at his optimum potential and remain alert for impending danger against his flock. Therefore, how does the shepherd find rest? The shepherd would rest while the sheep were by the river quenching their thirst. That is why David alluded to the still waters and the restoring of his soul. He would lay on the grass and rest. In agriculture, there is a law that the land should rest for a year so that the soil would replenish the nutrients needed to grow healthy plants. The Hebrew culture embraced and practiced this law and in the year of Jubilee, the land rested for a year (Exod. 23: 10-11).

When you become weary and tired while taking care of those around you, and serving as God want you to, there is a place that you can go to find rest and solace. Jesus Christ said we can go to him.

> *Come to me, all you who are weary and burdened, and I will give you rest. Take my yoke upon you, and learn from me, for I am gentle and humble in heart: and you will find rest for your souls (Matt. 11:28-29).*

Jesus extends an invitation to the weary traveler who is thirsty and fatigued by this world's troubles and the demands of ministry. We need to take time to rest awhile from the maddening and demanding crowd so that we can receive restoration for the next leg of the journey. To attempt to continue the journey without receiving revival and sustenance is to engage in self-sabotage. God did not call us to save anyone since He said that is the Holy Spirit's work to draw men to Him. Our responsibility is to be faithful and obedient servants of His word. When we try to take the place of the Holy Spirit in the lives of men, or the Church, then that is when we operate in our strength and the flesh would fail us.

If you are carrying a yoke or the burden of being a pleaser of men or seeking the validation of your peers and the crowd, you will become weary, and it would be swift and furious. However, if you seek to please God and crave His approval, you will not grow weary and frustrated doing His will or functioning in your calling and life's vocation. Instead, you will find rest, peace, joy, and fulfillment, knowing that you are in the center of His plans, and nothing can move you from that position.

Resting assumes the stance of Mary the mother of Jesus when the angel visited her and she knew she would carry the promised Messiah in her womb. Not knowing how it will happen, how Joseph would respond and the pushback from her community she responded affirmatively.

> I am the Lord's servant," Mary answered. "May your word to me be fulfilled." (Luke 1:38).

And after she responded with obedience, she rested

> But Mary treasured up all these things and pondered them in her heart (Luke 2:19).

I believe it takes unlimited grace and faith to rest after a revelation like the one Mary received. How many times have you received a word or report which shakes your world and tests your character, when everyone including you expects a peaceful response, but you find it difficult to attain the peace you desire? Resting at that time will come from a place of full assurance about who God is and what

He can do. Knowing without a doubt that He is who He says He is. **ALL MIGHTY GOD!**

> *And Mary said: "my soul glorifies the Lord and my spirit rejoices in God my Saviour." (Luke 1: 46-47).*

Mary declared God to be who He said He is and affirmed His sovereignty. She rested in that belief and birthed the **Song of the Magnificat** also called a **canticle** or **Song of Mary** that is also incorporated into the liturgical worship of the Catholic and Eastern Orthodox churches. Rest in the God who created you, the one who knows your beginning and ending. The one who called you and positioned you for greatness. When you do that, you will not be anxious about life's disappointments or trials.

CHOOSE JOY

Finding joy in the most challenging circumstances is a choice for everyone. Joy as an expression of happiness is contagious. I remember receiving a phone call from one of my aunts during one of my regular quiet mornings when all I wanted to do was relax. I thought she called for something important and as we got talking, I began laughing. After enquiring about her reason for calling, she said she just wanted to hear my laughter. She told me that since I was a child, I would laugh just the way I was laughing presently. I occasionally heard stories from other family members about how I would laugh, clap and sing, and my maternal grandmother would laugh and say, *"Sing for me girl, sing."* When sadness started creeping into my life, I asked God to renew that joy and laughter, and He did. I love to laugh, sometimes I laugh at myself or the craziest of anything. I decided to choose joy. I began to celebrate events and milestones with the simplest of parties.

I will play music, sing karaoke, or bake a cake. Anything to make the time special. I do it because life is too short, and we do not have time on our hands.

Paul in Philippians 4:4 tells us to *"Rejoice in the Lord always. I will say it again: Rejoice!"* That was said to the Church at Philippi while he was encouraging them to give thanks and pray at all times. The act of rejoicing was not conditional, nor did it require a special event or act.

> *Consider it pure joy, my brothers and sisters, whenever you face trials of many kinds, because you know that the testing of your faith produces perseverance. Let perseverance finish its work so that you may be mature and complete, not lacking anything (James 1:2-4).*

Paul specified an attitude that should pervade even the most difficult and exacting circumstances of life. Now there must be a rationale for that imperative. Is it because joy gives strength?

> *…. Do not grieve, for the joy of the Lord is your strength* (Neh. 8:10).

The children of Israel were in a season of restoration and as Ezra the scribe read from the scrolls to them, they understood how much they grieved God because of their sin and rebellion. However, God signaled to them that help was on the way and He was going to change their circumstances. He still loved them despite their disobedience. God commanded them to eat, drink, give to their neighbors, make merry, rejoice, and experience true joy because restoration was on the way (Neh. 8: 1-10).

The prophet Habakkuk resolved to choose joy after being perplexed and angry about the persecution of his people by the Assyrians who held them in captivity. He pleaded with God to deliver them. God responded to Habakkuk that there was an appointed time before He delivered them. He gave Habukkuk instructions to write the vision until God was ready to deliver His people. Eventually, the prophet changed his disposition from one of complaint to one of rejoicing. He affirmed:

> *Though the fig tree does not bud and there are no grapes on the vines, though the olive crop fails and the fields produce no food, though there are no sheep in the pen and no cattle in the stalls, yet I will rejoice in the LORD, I will be joyful in God my Savior (Hab. 3: 17-18).*

Choose to rejoice as Habakkuk did. You must believe the report of the Lord and not cling to what your eyes see that seems impossible (Num. 13:26-31; Isa.53:1) because after mourning there will be rejoicing. Your weeping is only for a season and there is also a season for rejoicing, but you must embrace it (Ps. 30:5; Eccles. 3:4) You cannot and will not weep forever.

> *Those who sow with tears will reap with songs of joy (Psalm 126:5).*

The lack of joy affects the body. What is holding back your joy?

> *A happy heart makes the face cheerful, but heartache crushes the spirit (Prov. 15:13).*

Continual sadness and sorrow, if not managed, are detrimental to the human body. What is holding back your joy?

*A cheerful heart is good medicine: but a crushed spirit
dries up the bones (Prov. 17:22).*

Jesus' desire for us is that we must be full of joy and that we must
do everything to protect and keep that joy. **YOU DESERVE TO
HAVE JOY IN YOUR LIFE.**

*I have told you this so that my joy may be in you and that
your joy may be complete (John 15:11).*

*I am coming to you now, but I say these things while I am
still in the world, so that they may have the full measure
of my joy within them (John 17:13).*

Joy and laughter are characteristics of God (Ps. 2: 4). We are made
in His image and likeness, which is not an outward expression, but
the essence of God's nature. We are God's *Imago Dei*. God's image-
bearers are made in His image and likeness to represent Him. Since
that is the case, we also carry our heavenly Father's DNA. His joy is
that we express His nature on the earth, which includes joy and happiness. That disposition comes only from a place of knowing Him,
His power in our lives, and the strength He provides through joy.

You must make that decision about entertaining joy in your life. It
will not happen without effort but must be a priority in daily activities. Create the time to celebrate the people and good things in your
life. What you do not have control of, leave it in God's hands and
trust him completely.

Trusting, being grateful, resting, and choosing joy are important
principles to strengthen your faith in your new experience at home
with the Lord. You can recline and exhale in the embrace of the love
that will not let you go. God desires that we walk in freedom.

Without healing, we would not be free, and we cannot celebrate our lives. He wants to set you free so that you can experience His joy. When you receive His joy it transfers to your relationship with others and impacts their response to you as well. **YES, JOY IS CONTAGIOUS AND INFECTIOUS!**

Conclusion

I n one of Jesus' conversations with his disciples after the indefatigable Simon Peter asked one of his numerous questions, Jesus responded that they may not understand what he was doing or saying, but eventually, they will (John 13:7). That is the life given to us. We do not know everything and never will. The truth is I do not think I want to know everything because that is just a lot of responsibility, and with responsibility comes accountability. Neither do we have all the answers and never will. Paul endorsed our limitation in the knowledge of what God will do and how He will do it.

> *For we know in part, and we prophesy in part. but when completeness comes, what is in part disappears (I Cor. 13:9-10).*

While we are limited in our knowledge, God expects us to trust Him and rest in His promises and love for us. When we turn our hearts to God that is what happens; we trust, we grow, and we develop strength. Moses felt limited in his ability to lead the Hebrews out of Egyptian bondage when directed by God. He knew he was called and what he had to do but felt inadequate for the mission. Then God reassured him that He will direct and guide him.

The Lord himself goes before you and will be with you; he will never leave you nor forsake you. Do not be afraid; do not be discouraged (Deut. 31:8).

I remember as a child when I attended elementary school. I was somewhere between ages five and eight years. When the school bell rang in the afternoon to signal the end of the school day, we all shouted, "YAAAAAAAY!" All students gave that shout for one reason only. It was time to go home. There was so much excitement as we grabbed our bags and lunch kits and rushed through the doors and out of the gate. Sometimes we forgot that the teacher was in the classroom and had to dismiss us. As punishment for not following the dismissal rules, we returned to our seats until we did what was right or stayed an extra five minutes. Whatever happened, one thing stood out in my mind, and that was the excitement to get home. That excitement meant we would be able to end a stressful day and get to a place of safety, love, and peace.

When I used the word **HOME** in this book, it denoted both a symbolic and spiritual meaning as a place of love, security, peace, hope, and purpose. A place of acceptance, without judgment, understanding without questioning motives, and being embraced without rejection. I knew what the experience meant for me and how it changed my view of the experiences I encountered. I know how it renewed my faith. I know first-hand how it restored my health. And I know how much I treasure the experience and place where I am now at home with God in my heart and spirit. To renew purpose, to walk in the divine pathway God destined for me without fear, inhibition, or restraint, is a blessing beyond comparison, and God wants the same for you also.

So if the Son sets you free, you will be free indeed (John 8:36).

What do you want God to do for you? There was a man who Jesus asked that question. He was blind and sitting on the roadway while Jesus passed by. Jesus heard him calling out and asked him the question (Mark 10:46-52). Today Jesus is also asking you that question. Do you have an answer? I hope you do, because if you don't, how will you receive what you need for your journey? You will be like the prodigal son who sits in the pigpen eating the pig's food not remembering that his father's table had a big spread with various delicacies, waiting for him to partake. All he had to do was go and take what he wanted without asking. Your table is spread, ready, and waiting for you. I also want you to experience the fulness of God's blessings and grace in your life so that you can be restored and healed through the power of God. Do not be afraid, God will be with you (Josh. 1:9). His grace will sustain you in your trials and weaknesses, and you will receive strength as you surrender to His will (2 Cor. 12:9).

God is calling you home to Himself and wants to occupy a prominent place in your life. He wants to love and take care of you because he has already provided all that you need for your earthly and heavenly existence (2 Pet. 1:3). You will not lack anything when you walk into a relationship with Jesus Christ. My prayer is that you will answer the call to return to God if you are estranged from Him. If you do not know Him as your personal Lord and indwelling Saviour, make Him the Lord of your life. As you respond to the love that calls you home, He will restore hope and your life will be fulfilling.

> *Being confident of this, that he who began a good work in you will carry it on to completion until the day of Christ Jesus (Phil. 1:6).*

God will complete what He started in you, and you must believe that. The journey may be difficult, but He will bring you to that place of your pre-ordained destiny.

WHEN LOVE CALLS YOU HOME

Wandering, lost, and searching for hope
Battered, bruised, hurting, and confused
Reaching forth to grasp the truth
The truth of where I am now and where I must go
Just simply longing for peace, to be free, asking earnestly
When will love call me home?

The cries left unheard
The calls for help reached beneath my core
A yearning desire for change
To understand the journey
And make sense of my pain
Which I know can only subside
In the safety of love's call to go home

To hold hope against my chest
And know that God is guiding my steps
Gently leading to paths unknown
It is a journey of restoration and healing
In the Father's presence finding rest
Leading me to love, which I know will carry me home

And there in my questions and longing to be free
Like a trapped bird released from a cage
I felt love's wooing a call to come home
I leaped from the place where captive I lay
I soar gently to love's endearing embrace
Answering the call of love's gentle wooing
To my Saviour and Lord, I feel safe from the storm
There in that place of timeless grace
WHEN LOVE CALLED ME HOME

Anne-Marie L. James-Henry © 2021

Notes

Bibliography

Bible Hub. (2021). Philippians 2 in *Bible Commentaries*. Retrieved on November 5, 2020, from https://biblehub.com/commentaries/philippians/2-5.htm

James, A. (2009). *The Seasons of Your Life*. Trinidad and Tobago. R & I Advertising.

Henry, M. (2021). Acts 17 in *Matthew Henry's Commentary on the Whole Bible*. Bible Hub. Retrieved December 10, 2020, from https://biblehub,com/commentaries/mhcw/ acts/17.htm

Jackson-Cherry, L. R., & Erford, B. T. (2014). *Crisis assessment, intervention, and prevention* (3rd ed.). New York. Pearson.

Maxwell, J. C. (2010). *Everyone Communicates, Few Connect: What The Most Effective People Do Differently*. Nashville. Thomas Nelson.

Merriam-Webster. (n.d.). Calibrate. *In Merriam-Webster.com dictionary*. Retrieved November 10, 2020, from https://www.merriam-webster.com/dictionary/ calibrate

Merriam-Webster. (n.d.). Connection. *In Merriam-Webster.com dictionary*. Retrieved December 12, 2020, from https://www.merriam-webster.com/ dictionary/connection

Merriam-Webster. (n.d.). Conviction. *In Merriam-Webster.com dictionary*. Retrieved October 19, 2020, from https://www.merriam-webster.com/ dictionary/conviction

Merriam-Webster. (n.d.). Crisis. *In Merriam-Webster.com dictionary*. Retrieved October 19, 2020, from https://www.merriam-webster.com/dictionary/crisis

Merriam-Webster. (n.d.). Healing. *In Merriam-Webster.com dictionary*. Retrieved March 9, 2021, from https://www.merriam-webster.com/dictionary/healing

Merriam-Webster. (n.d.). Re. *In Merriam-Webster.com dictionary*. Retrieved November 10, 2020, from https://www.merriam-webster.com/dictionary/re

Merriam-Webster. (n.d.). Rest. *In Merriam-Webster.com dictionary*. Retrieved January 12, 2021, from https://www.merriam-webster.com/dictionary/rest

Merriam-Webster. (n.d.). Restoration. *In Merriam-Webster.com dictionary*. Retrieved March 9, 2020, from https://www.merriam-webster.com/dictionary/restoration

Merriam-Webster. (n.d.). Trust. *In Merriam-Webster.com dictionary*. Retrieved January 12, 2020, from https://www.merriam-webster.com/dictionary/trust

Van Der Kolk, B. A. (2014). *The body keeps the score: Brain, mind, and body in the healing of trauma*. New York. Viking Press.

Walsh, Froma. (2009). *Spiritual Resources in Family Therapy*. (Second Edition). New York. Guilford Press.

About the Author

Anne-Marie is an author, speaker, pastor and marriage and family therapist who specializes in life transition issues. She loves to read, cook, write, listen to music and take nature walks as she communes with the Lord. Her heart is drawn to grace, forgiveness, justice, equality, and purposeful living.

This woman with a servants' heart is a licensed, credentialed minister with the Pentecostal Assemblies of the West Indies, Tobago District where she has held several positions of leadership over the twenty-one years of service before migrating to the United States. She attained a Bachelor's Degree in Theology from the West Indies School of Theology, Trinidad and Tobago, a Master's Degree in Christian Counseling from the Jacksonville Theological Seminary, Florida, and a Master's Degree in Marriage and Family Therapy from the Abilene Christian University, Texas, USA.

Anne-Marie has counseled many and worked with women, youths, children and families for over twenty years. She hosted local radio programs for women and children in Tobago. Was a featured speaker at women's conferences, youth conferences, and camps. Also facilitated training and life skills coaching in several areas of church ministry with individuals, groups, communities and churches during her travels. She was a certified mentor with the Government of Trinidad and Tobago, Ministry of National Security Mentorship Program.

This servant of God was an assistant pastor of the PAWI Abundant Life Missions Church Signal from 2006-2015. A lecturer at the West Indies School of Theology, Tobago Off Campus from 2002-2015. Facilitator and Supervisor at Life at the Crossroads, values education program with Family Life Tobago in Secondary School from 2005 to 2015.

Anne-Marie is a wife, mother, daughter, sister, friend, confidante, motivator, life skills coach and military spouse. She is currently a Licensed Graduate Marriage and Family Therapist in the State of Maryland where she resides with her family.

Anne-Marie's Social Media

Facebook: www.facebook.com/annemarie.james.31

Instagram: www.instagram.com/annemariejameshenry/feed/

LinkedIn: www.linkedin.com/in/anne-marie-l-james-henry -lgmft-mmft-mcc-71958041

Endnotes

1   The journey here is meant to convey both an actual and figurative meaning. Journey | Definition sourced by Merriam-Webster (merriam-webster.com)

2   Healing | Definition of Healing by Merriam-Webster (merriam-webster.com)

3   Restoration | Definition of Restoration by Merriam-Webster (merriam-webster.com)

4   Re | Definition of Re by Merriam-Webster (merriam-webster.com)

5   Storing | Definition of Storing by Merriam-Webster (merriam-webster.com)

6   Other definitions include: contingency, crossroad, turning point. You can find more information in Crisis | Definition of Crisis by Merriam-Webster (merriam-webster.com)

7   Other definitions include: assurance, certitude, confidence, sureness, surety, opinion, belief, persuasion, view, dogma. Conviction | Definition of Conviction by Merriam-Webster (merriam-webster.com)

8   In a crisis there are some crtical steps. Writing from this author will assist with practical steps you can implement for yourself and in your work with others.(Jackson-Cherry & Erford, 2014)

9   Pottery making is a unique craft which demands skill and a depth of patience. Reading some of this information will help you adjust your thinking about Gods' role in our live s to bring us to wholeness. I hope that you will find the study rewarding.Pottery Making: An Introduction- Pottery Making Info

[10]   Arc eyes is a condition when there is inflammation of the cornea.

[11]   The author presents a comprehensive view of trauma and the impact on bodily functions. He observes how the body readjusts to manage the trauma and the subsequent imact on triggers. See the following site for more information (PDF) The Body Keeps the Score: Memory and the Evolving Psychobiology of Posttraumatic Stress (researchgate.net)

[12]   To obtain more information about brain activity and how one can change one's thinking or rearrange information about trauma you can visit the works of the author.(Van der Kolk, 2014)

[13]   Arrow - Wikipedia provides a comprehensive description on the use of the arrow.

[14]   Information sourced from the Webster's dictionary that provides the etymology of the word pavilion. The basic idea is a covering or a place of shelter.

[15]   Calibrate | Definition of Calibrate by Merriam-Webster (merriam-webster.com)

[16]   Defining Love in the Bible: Greek Agape, Phileo, Eros, Storge (gods-word-first.org)

[17]   Acts 17 Matthew Henry's Commentary on the Whole Bible (biblehub.com)

[18]   This book will help you with fostering healthy connections and how you can communicate to connect. Everyone Communicates, Few Connect by John C. Maxwell - Bing video

[19]   Connection | Definition of Connection by Merriam-Webster (merriam-webster.com)

[20]   I found this an enlightening research on the root meaning of the word connection. It tells me there can be no connection without association and you cannot have a one man association. Social connection is important. How to say connection in Greek (wordhippo.com)

[21]   Source of the definition of the greek word connection - Bing

22   Trust | Definition of Trust by Merriam-Webster (merriam-webster.com)

23   This reference explains the experience of Hagar which led to the naming of the place where she heard from God. "El Roi" Meaning and Importance: The God Who Sees Me (biblestudytools.com)

24   Sometimes we use saying and do not understand their origin. Knowing the origin provides more depth to your expression of the saying. Do some research of some of your favorites sayings and you will find it refreshing and enriching. 'Home is where the heart is' - Origin, Meaning, Explanation and Importance of the Proverb - ImportantIndia.com

25   Rest | Definition of Rest by Merriam-Webster (merriam-webster.com)

CPSIA information can be obtained
at www.ICGtesting.com
Printed in the USA
BVHW042320261022
650444BV00004B/19